SUCCESSFUL CHILDREN

by

RAYMOND T. COPPOLA

Walker and Company
NEW YORK

To my Mother and Father
Ida and Chris Coppola

First published in the United States of America in 1978 by the Walker Publishing Company, Inc.

Published simultaneously in Canada by Beaverbooks, Limited, Pickering, Ontario.

Cloth ISBN: 0-8027-9051-8
Paper ISBN: 0-8027-7129-7

Library of Congress Catalog Card Number: 77-78374

Printed in the United States of America

10 9 8 7 6 5 4 3 2 1

Contents

Foreword

To have and to raise a family is a complex, demanding process. The child-raising experience increases in complexity with each year of growth and reaches a crescendo when the child enters school. New, often unexpected, requirements and demands are placed on the child, who must leave his known world and enter the new world of the school. The child must now integrate the learning from home life with the many new problems that school life presents. The success of the child's school life depends greatly on the experiences he has had at home. Thus, adults in the home and the school must be knowledgeable and supportive of each other to make the elementary school years the time of vibrant living and learning.

Parents and all adults interested in and concerned about the education of children have long needed a book that sets forth clearly the best that is now known about helping the child to achieve success and joy in learning. Recent research shows that there is a distinct relationship between success in school and the involvement of the home in the learning process. In the past, the school has seldom encouraged the family of the child to participate in the teaching-learning process. As a result, not enough about the world of the school and its course of study is known to them. This book, with its comprehensive review of the school's typical course of study at each grade level, will enable all the adults who interact personally with children to work together to develop motivation and study habits that can enable the child to succeed. The manual of activities will develop in the child just the right combination of confidence and curiosity to bring to every learning situation.

Reading is an essential tool for success in our society. Children must read. One of the reasons why many children do not read adequately is that today's child has less opportunity to practice reading. We do best what we do most. This book supplies interesting and enjoyable activities designed to make reading become an integral part of the child's daily life at home and at school. All the skills necessary for reading are presented in a game format which allows them to make sense to the child. As a result, the skills will be remembered and be available for use when needed. Reading thus becomes one of the most important ways a child can meet his needs and widen his interests.

Television has frequently been described as the "American child's third parent." Estimates of how much time children spend watching television vary, but the evidence is clear that most children spend several hours a day in front of their sets. It is important for adults to understand the messages being transmitted by television if they are to help children know how to make the best use of it. Ray Coppola presents a balanced view of television and then provides ideas that will help the child become a critical television viewer. He suggests activities for making television viewing supportive of the reading process and thus enable parents to make television viewing time an experience for positive, active learning.

Throughout the book, Mr. Coppola systematically presents an approach to the teaching-learning process that will develop in children an appreciation of the fact that, although every child has the right to an *education*, it is each child's own responsibility actually to learn.

Successful Children thus provides an urgently needed means to unite children, parents and teachers of all kinds in a common enterprise that will be both agreeable and productive for everyone concerned.

—Deirdre Breslin, Ph.D.
Professor of Education
FORDHAM UNIVERSITY

Introduction

As the pace of modern life has gotten faster and more complicated, it has become increasingly difficult for children to enjoy the learning process as an integral part of growing up. Children who *can* make it, simply *don't*. They flounder, they are bored, their grades are nothing to write home about. Few are excited by learning. Few reach their potential. As a concerned parent, can you help your child learn faster, learn more efficiently, and love every minute of it? Can you help him to be successful in school, confident, enthusiastic, and more creative?* You bet you can.

You are one of your child's greatest assets. You can introduce him to the tools of his future trade. You can reinforce the learning experience and make it real, make it fun, make it stick. Education is everywhere—not just in the schools. When simple, everyday home experiences expand your child's interest and intelligence, he will begin to succeed in school and begin to find "learning" everywhere.

The easy-to-follow instructions and techniques described in this book will not require hours of your time or skills you don't have. Many of the activities can be done in the course of the usual time you spend with your child. Other activities will be ones that you will direct your child toward, for exploration on his own. He can be inspired to use his time better, to see things more clearly, to understand the usefulness of what he learns and its application to his very own world.

---

*Pronouns "he", "him", and "his" will be used for both boys and girls throughout the book.

1

By using this book, you as a parent will find out how to give positive reinforcement to your child's learning experiences, how to get the most out of family conversations and activities, how to help your child use and enjoy the public library, television, books, newspapers, dictionaries, games, songs, and day-to-day routines. You will understand exactly what he is learning in school at each level, and you will have specific activities to do with him at home. Your rapport and communication with your child will increase. Learning will once again be fun—for both of you. And you can have the deep satisfaction of helping your child to be successful instead of lost, to achieve, to enjoy, to move rapidly in his learning, to accept responsibility, to reach the fullest extent of his own marvelous potential. You can help your child to be the best he can be, to grow into a person you and he will be proud of, to open doors to an exciting and fulfilling future.

There have been many people who have given me assistance and encouragement during my research and writing. Those in the field of education include Dr. Dorothy Strickland, Dr. James Hills, Dr. Linnea Weiland, Mr. Joseph Bermudez, M.S.W., Ms. Norma Mingo, Ms. Evelyn Austin, Ms. Louise Gemake, Mr. Frank Wohlfort, Ms. Loyda Alfalla, Ms. Susan Sheen, Ms. Irene Kearsley Billips and Ms. Anna Rodriguez for her assistance in typing the manuscript.

My deep appreciation to Ms. Carol Lea Benjamin for her assistance in editing the manuscript and special thanks to Mr. Richard Winslow, who served as my editor at Walker Book Company, for his time, patience and guidance in the preparation of the book.

For their encouragement and belief in the project thanks must go to my brother, Bob Coppola, my sister and brother-in-law, Marilyn and John Niedzinski, and my friends Nadine Sasek, Nelson Rosabal, Patricia Bold, James McCarthy, Jim Wynns and Nick Russo. My friend and counselor, Jim Campise, Esq., deserves special mention for his reading of and advice concerning the manuscript.

—Raymond T. Coppola

1

Successful Children

Who is the successful child? How can he be recognized? How is he superior to his peers? What makes him tick? Success in school, which is often the forerunner to success in life, can be spotted by both objective and subjective criteria. Look in on any classroom scene. Some children are bored; they look around the room lethargically or daydream about being elsewhere. Others try to "hide" from the teacher. They may feel inadequate, unsure of themselves, even alienated. Too many feel obliged to vie for the teacher's attention by displays of negative behavior.

The successful child feels confident in his environment, whether he's in school, out playing with friends, or at home with his parents and siblings. He is curious, alive, aware. He is the child in school who raises his hand enthusiastically when he has a question or an answer. He participates, he cooperates, he partakes and enjoys. He is willing to take chances, and he is not afraid to offer an opinion or ask a question. He likes his teachers, within reason, and enjoys school. He is the child any teacher will remember and is the reason that teachers enjoy teaching. He absorbs, he offers feedback. He shares both his knowledge and his enthusiasm with the group.

His curiosity is alive in settings other than school, as well. He may collect stamps or study birds. Perhaps he excels in sports. He is active rather than passive. He does things on his own. He rarely, if ever, gets bored. He moves with greater ease through new situations, taking from them all there is to be taken. He is more cooperative at home because he is confident in himself. He is both interested and interest-

3

ing. He is not difficult to spot because he is the child who shines in any setting.

Your child spends only 180 days a year in school. During the 6 hours in each school day only about 4 hours are spent on actual instruction. For the vast amount of knowledge your child is required to learn, he has less than 800 hours of instruction per year. His teacher has twenty-five to thirty-five children in the class. Working alone, she must teach all the children to read, write, communicate, and learn facts, skills, and insights relating to literature, science, math, social studies, music, and art. Time for individual instruction and personal contact is necessarily limited by the structure of the system. Yet many children, those with a special edge, make it in this situation. Your child doesn't have to be left to sink or swim on his own. You are with your child for long periods of time, and the time you spend with him can be put to productive and enjoyable use. You can reinforce your child's school learning while you are together outdoors, shopping in the supermarket, working in the kitchen or in the garden. In the living room, on walks, and on trips in the car he can use his mind and his senses to profit him as a student. By taking advantage of normal, everyday situations and opportunities, you can positively reinforce your child's learning in an informal manner. You can help your child to become a successful child.

Perhaps your child has been pigeonholed in school as a B or C student. You can help him break the pattern by encouraging his interests. He can learn to participate if his confidence to ask and answer questions is stimulated and encouraged at home. He can bring to school projects he does at home and surprise his teachers with his new interests. He will learn to be more aware in any environment. His subjective feelings about himself will improve as he searches successfully for knowledge. But there will be positive objective feedback also, to keep him stimulated and motivated. His grades will improve. His status in the classroom will improve. After all, in school success is the name of the game. All these factors can have a positive effect on his psychological development, social maturity, and intellectual growth. You, his parent and the most important individual in his life, can have a hand in raising his feelings of self-esteem and satisfaction. This book can help release the untapped force between parent and child that can make all the difference in school performance. You will see how easy and pleasant it can be to help your own child be more successful. The results will thrill you both.

But why should you take a part in your child's education? You are busy, perhaps overworked; you have other interests and need time to yourself. After all, isn't education the job of the schools?

President Harry S Truman used to have a sign on his desk saying, The Buck Stops Here. Your child has certain responsibilities in school, and certainly so do his teachers. But ultimately, credit or blame will fall on you as his parent. Though some brilliant, perceptive educator may inspire your child to be a creative genius, she will not be long remembered. Nor will any one teacher be looked at askance if your child turns out to be a failure. No one would seriously suggest that parents replace teachers or the school system. Nor would anyone suggest that children abdicate responsibility for their education. On the contrary, the methods described in this book will engender more responsibility in your son or daughter. Herein, a plea for less buck passing and more responsibility for children, with parents leading them toward the goal of being successful.

The teacher's role in education has long been clear: she must know her material and her students, help create an atmosphere conducive to education, inspire students, instruct them, and initiate productive behavior. For their part, the students must obey the rules and regulations, pay attention, and do their work, whether they like it or not. But what of the parental role in education? By initially taking on more responsibility in your child's education, you can inspire and teach your child to take responsibility himself. The interest you engender in him, the confidence you help build, and the skills you share will help your child to take charge of his life and his education. He will work because he wants to learn, not because he has to. He will work because it is fascinating to learn, not just in order to get an A or to avoid a D. The fact is that every child can't get A's. But he will learn what it means to be responsible instead of having a "let George do it" attitude. He will do his best.

How will he be changed by his new responsible attitudes? He may start with responsible initiative in taking care of his room or a pet. He will develop a sense of pride in the accomplishment of a job well done. This marvelous attitude can be a lifelong habit, an attitude that extends to his schoolwork, his relations with others, and eventually to his career. You will be able to help him take on jobs that he can do or that present a challenge he thinks he can meet. He will learn not to make and break foolish promises or set unrealistic goals. He will learn the consequences, good and bad, of responsibility and irresponsibility. And these points are the key factors for any successful person. As your child finds his "sea legs," as he learns what he can handle and what he can't, as he learns to expand his skills and knowledge, he will be a better companion and family member. He will learn to pull his own weight at home, too. He can and will become a participator, a joiner, a helper—all willingly and with joy—if he is led gently and thoughtfully by loving parents.

And since the goal of all education is independence, what greater gift can you offer your child than help toward that ultimate goal? You will be teaching him how to make decisions; how to find information; how to use his mind, his hands, and his senses; how to function in the kitchen, the library, the workroom, and in natural settings. All this can be done in the time you usually spend with him—and with more fun than effort. Who is the successful child? He can be your child.

Parent participation in a child's learning can help show a child the relevance to his life of what he learns in school. What can be more basic than the preparation and eating of food? Yet, simple mathematics and reading are needed in the kitchen in order to prepare food. And what could be a better example of solidifying the educational experience, of a perfect marriage between school and home, than parent and child cooking together? Here, in this life-essential activity, the theories, numbers, problems, and hard work of school become filled with rich meaning. Why learn numbers or how to read? It's simple—for survival, for joy. At every age children can help in the kitchen and can thus grow and learn without taking up too much of a busy parent's time. A youngster may start off peeling carrots (and counting the number of strokes per carrot) or mixing a batter (and reading the directions for baking the cake). As skills grow, so does confidence. What pride when the family shouts, "Who baked the bread? It's great!"

Through such activities learning becomes a living experience, full of fun and excitement. And from that excitement children can acquire a beautiful habit: the pursuit of knowledge. Such a desire can be a great influence on the child's success in school.

You need not buy a blackboard and chalk or try to become a teacher in order to help your child be successful. This goal is best accomplished when the three partners in your child's education each fulfill their own responsibilities. Your child, his teacher, and you each have an essential role in helping your child to be successful. You can make the world his classroom. You can show pride, love, and pleasure in his accomplishments in a way that no one else can. You can make learning personal and meaningful for your child. You can help him reach his potential and do his very best. You can help him be a successful child.

2

Working with Children

Children Are People

Children are people, and all people go through stages, moods, changes, regressions, periods of growth, periods of stagnation. Children develop at such a rapid pace that parents should expect to observe a whirlwind of change that can be as confusing to them as it is to the child. One day he'll want your constant attention and warmth. The next day he'll tell you to leave him alone. He may surprise you by coming home with library books and want to do nothing but read. Then for two days he'll just want to play with his friends.

This is all part of the developmental process, in which children are learning and searching for their role in life. Don't let these vicissitudes upset you. Try to accept them for what they are. Raising a child is a difficult task. A good sense of humor can help every parent get through the difficult moments.

A Matter of Interest

Why is it that so many of our school-age children do not enjoy learning? They go through the motions like robots from nine to three. They appear to be lifeless, dull, bored, unobservant, restless, and uncommitted. Then, at three fifteen, they are suddenly catapulted back into life. In the school yard or park they are full of determination, enthusiasm, interest, energy, and life. What causes this Dr. Jekyll–Mr. Hyde transformation to come about?

Why, if children can recite the programs in the *TV Guide* without difficulty, can't they read their textbooks well? Why can't children remember the names of the oceans or the planets, when they can tell you the names and positions of all the players of their favorite sports teams? Why?

The reason is simple and obvious. Learning is greatly affected by interest levels. When a child is interested in the subject matter, learning takes place naturally. When the subject matter seems boring and unimportant, learning becomes a matter of tedious work.

Repetition is another factor that enables children to learn enthusiastically about the things they like. Children, like adults, talk about the things they are interested in. From these conversations, as well as from the television and reading material that relate to the things they are interested in, they acquire more and more knowledge about a favorite topic. The newly discovered information is easily learned because the knowledge they have already acquired serves as a basis to relate the new information to. The facts no longer exist in a vacuum but rather are meaningfully joined to the child's past knowledge.

Test this theory out for yourself. During dinner ask your child what he learned in school today. Most often the answer will be hesitant, unexciting, short, and uncaring. He may even say, "Nothing." Now pick a topic that you know interests your child, such as dolls, sports, monsters, fishing, a new dress, or a favorite television show. With the right leading questions to spur his imagination you will have your child talking endlessly, excitedly, and full of interest and enthusiasm. And by being aware of what your child is learning in the school subject areas, you can include all these areas in the conversation.

Enjoyment

Besides interest, another important element in the learning process is enjoyment. When your child tells you in dull tones that he has to do a book report for a class project but can't think of anything he wants to do it on, direct him to books that have to do with areas of fun and excitement to him. If he is a sports enthusiast, suggest biographies of his sports heroes. If she likes dolls, show her *Alice in Wonderland.* Her report can include her own illustrations of a modern Alice representation in doll clothes. Does your child like animals? Direct him to the numerous good books of wildlife stories that are appealing and popular for almost all ages.

Caring

When you show interest in your child's schoolwork, you show him that you care. Through that interest you can further develop the bonds of love and the values of a one-to-one relationship. You make him feel important. You show your interest by reading to him, by helping him with his more difficult work, by spurring him on to be the very best he can be. By being concerned about the things that concern him—without placing a value judgment on those concerns—you accept him as the individual that he is and enable him to be comfortable with himself. No parent has all the answers for any child, no parent can be everything to the child at all times, and no parent can insulate the child from the many problems, fears, trials, and tribulations that all individuals face as they grow into adulthood. You can, however, make your child feel secure and comfortable with himself by accepting him, by taking a real interest in his interests, by being supportive through easy and difficult times, through the growths and the regressions that are a part of his personality development—by caring.

Praise

When you praise your child for his work, when you tell him how well he is doing, when you tell him how proud you are of his work, you make him feel the same way adults feel when they get a raise, a promotion, a successful report, or a bonus. Of course, false praise isn't good for anyone, least of all children, but think of how long you would keep doing your best at your job if your efforts were not rewarded in some way by your boss and you will understand the importance of praise for children.

Did your daughter get an A in math on her report card? Tell Aunt Kay about it in her presence the next time you are visiting. Did your son get a good part in the school play? Invite some friends to join you in seeing him in his acting debut and then surprise him with a party afterward. Let your child know through your actions that he or she is the most important individual on earth to you. Your child will return that feeling to you tenfold.

Discipline

No one enjoys discipline, but everyone must experience it. So when you have to discipline your child, do it promptly and get it over with. Then you can get on to something else. Disciplining children is a personal matter. Parents must decide for themselves how to handle it. It's important to be firm and consistent but also to see things in proper perspective. Try to let the punishment fit the transgression. If your child's transgression is not over anything really big, be direct and firm in telling him that he had better not do it again. If he repeats an unpleasant action or neglects his chores repeatedly, stronger discipline might be called for. Be sure your child knows *why* he is being punished and that he truly understands the necessity of the punishment. In this way he will learn from the experience, and hopefully there will be no repeat performance.

Correcting Your Child

Discipline is actually an easy matter; it is done and over with. Correcting your child for little habits that annoy you or put you on edge can become a tedious limitation to the enjoyment of a good parent-child relationship. Don't fall into the trap of being so annoyed at such behavior that your child learns that the way to get your goat is simply to leave the toothpaste cap off the tube. Make your corrective advice rather matter-of-fact. Once it's done, it's done. Be fair, be consistent. Don't leave your child hanging, but make up when your point has gotten through. Don't let him feel bad about himself for something minor. Try to know your own feelings. If you find there's too much steam over a small situation, back off and cool down. Again, your sense of humor can go a long way in helping your child to correct his bad habits.

Rules and Routines

Children want structure because they need it. They don't want to be hounded or nagged, and they certainly don't want to be treated like babies, but they want direction from their parents. And with that direction they want to know *why*. Set the rules and stick to them. Whether they concern curfews, television time, study time, or household responsibilities, make sure your child knows them and keeps them. And when transgressions take place, do something about them. This doesn't mean that flexibility should not be in order for a television special, a special event, or as a reward for work well done. It does mean that all children need guidance and direction from their parents. They need to know that lines must be drawn, that structure exists.

What Your Child Learns in School

The most important thing any child can learn in school is to love learning. All too often, however, because of overcrowded classrooms, too much subject matter, and not enough stimulating activities that involve them in interesting and entertaining work, children become bored and turned off. Although they go through the motions of learning, their minds are really a hundred miles away.

First and foremost, learning requires paying attention to the subject matter. The standard elementary school curriculum comprises the major subject areas of language arts, math, social studies, and science, as well as the minor subject areas of art, music, and physical education. The four major curriculum areas are gradually developed throughout the grades in order to give the child a solid foundation that will enable him to expand them in junior high school, high school, and college. The most important curriculum area is language arts, in which he learns how to read, write, and communicate orally. Such skills are essential, for without them the child cannot get very far in life, nor can he learn any other subject areas. Without them he could not read the textbooks and reference material, write essays or exams, or communicate knowledge orally for science, social studies, or math. The child who is not a competent reader will normally have tremendous difficulty with most other subject areas simply because he cannot understand the material.

The language arts experience concerns the essential communication skills that are common to our daily experience. It is therefore the learning area that parents can most easily reinforce to help their children succeed in school! Every time your child asks the meaning of a word and you tell him, you are helping him in language arts. Every time you and your child discuss an area of interest to him, he is practicing his language arts skills in oral communication. Every time you read to your child, you reinforce his reading skills. The act of helping one's child be successful in school is not difficult, it is not time-consuming, and it is not tedious. Rather, it is easy, quick, and enjoyable for both parent and child. It is always successful when the parent accepts the child for what he is, beginning at the child's level of development, and not at the level at which the parent expects the child to be.

A Word About Potential

Potential is a funny word. Any parent who has more than one child is acutely aware of the differences between children. One child might love to read and write, the other might love to work with his hands. One might be quiet, whereas the other is the life of the party. One might be slow, when the other is fast. Some people are born with a genius mentality; others are born with mental, emotional, and physical deficiencies. The vast majority are somewhere in between. The potential of an individual is what he is able to accomplish at any given time. A child of eight does not usually have the potential to jump as far as a child of ten, simply because his body muscles have not developed enough. To judge the eight-year-old with the expectation that he has the same ability as the ten-year-old is unfair. And two eight-year-olds will also have different abilities for jumping. Winning is not the most important criterion for the child. What is healthy and what is important is that each child jumps as far as *he* can. And whenever a child does his very best, he is successful. Working with children means walking a narrow line between the two realms of either expecting too much from them or not expecting enough from them. When we expect too little, the child easily becomes bored and lethargic, lazy and inactive. When we expect too much, the child can become overwhelmed, turned off, fearful, and insecure. How can parents best walk this line? They must proceed very carefully, with tender loving care as their guide.

The best way to find out where your child is in terms of his ability level is by listening to him, by talking to his teacher, and by watching him react to the things he is doing. When he reads a particular book, watch to see if he is uncomfortable, see how many words he misses, see if he wants to read it or if it is a laborious task for him. If he is really struggling, direct him to other books that he can be more comfortable with. Don't worry about the fact that they may represent a reading level that is one or two levels below his grade level. *The important thing is that he is reading!* If he reads enough and is happy and interested in the subject matter, his reading level will progress naturally. When this occurs, your child will develop confidence in his ability to learn. Confidence, as we all know, is one of the cornerstones of success in anything. Don't overexert him and don't baby him; rather, use your own common sense in helping him achieve to his greatest potential.

Educating the Whole Child

Is television ever more important than homework? Is outdoor play ever more important than working on a term project? Yes, but the parent is the one who must make the decision concerning these matters. All work and no play makes Jack and Jill very dull children, and the goal of education is certainly not to create knowledgeable, dull children. Has he been working indoors too long? Send him out to play, or take him on a nature walk in the woods (see pages 166-169). When there is an important television special that would interest him and would give him information that you deem important, let him do his homework during the commercials. There are so many commercials that he will probably finish it before the show is over anyway. Have you seen a movie that is restricted but that you feel would nevertheless be beneficial to his growth, even though there are scenes in it that you do not like? Maybe he should see it, with you explaining to him why you want him to see the movie and what you object to in it as well.

The Greeks upheld the proposition of "a sound body and a sound mind." By introducing your child to a sport of his liking, you can help him develop his physical abilities as well. Of course, some children just aren't interested in athletics, but with today's wide range of sports—from tennis to ice skating to gymnastics—most children can become interested in a particular sport. Participating in a sport not only ensures physical activity but can be a great socializing experience for the child as well. And who knows? With a little natural ability, a few dollars spent on lessons, and a real liking for the sport, perhaps your child can win a scholarship to college, thereby saving you thousands of dollars in tuition. Being competent in a particular sport can be a great learning experience for your child in competitive behavior, self-composure when winning and losing, fair play, confidence, self-esteem, and determination.

Everyone has to grow up on his own and make his own mistakes. You can stand by your child through thick and thin, but you can't make all his decisions for him. Children have to live their own lives, and in that growth process they are going to come across both good and bad experiences. Loving a child often tempts parents to do the work for him or to try to insulate him. When they succeed in this, they have cheated their child out of a life experience, which involves work as well as play, bad times as well as good times. They only make it more difficult for their child in his later years to adjust to responsibilities, to the ups and downs of life. Don't fall into this trap with your child. Let him experience all of life as every individual should. You can be ready when he needs your help, without depriving him of life's full experience.

Speaking to Your Child

Throughout the elementary school years children develop their use of language to a vast extent. The next time you are conversing with your child, use a few big words that he does not normally use. Instead of saying to him, "Look at that pretty flower," say something like, "Isn't that flower magnificent?" Explain to him what the word *magnificent* means, use it again a little later in the conversation, and you will see how the child naturally comes to use such words on his own. When we expect little from children, we will receive little in return. When we look at their ability as being unlimited, their outlook can amaze us.

Our words of encouragement and praise as well as our words of anger and resentment have a tremendous effect on how children feel about themselves. Through them we can make a child feel good, confident, well-adjusted, and secure within himself; just as through negative words and feelings adults can make a child feel insecure, confused, unhappy, and a failure. Everyone, at one time or another, has been witness to a situation in which one wrong word, even though stated accidentally, caused an interesting conversation to become a confusing or laborious argument or a breakdown in a relationship. Words can have an overwhelming effect on children, and parents should be aware of the damage their use of improper words can do to the child's feelings about himself.

When it happens that harsh words are expressed—as they must sometimes be in any close relationship—let the emotion pass, then tell your child what you really meant to say and that you meant no harm, just as you would do with a friend.

Actions Speak Louder Than Words

If we tell a child not to smoke and yet we smoke in front of him, he is not going to believe our words. He might not smoke, but that does not mean he will respect our words. When the words and actions of parents constantly say different things to the child, he will eventually lose faith in those words. When the words and actions of parents coincide, children learn proper behavior without difficulty.

Tender Loving Care

Fish need water, birds need air, flowers need the sun, and children need love. Without loving care from their parents, children can easily become failures. Love comes from a one-to-one relationship that is founded on understanding, respect, warmth, caring, sharing, and laughing. A wink, a smile, a kiss, a warm hug, or an arm around the shoulder can result in what can be described as an electric current of life—a pizzazz, an "up," an irreplaceable communion of love between parent and child.

When you are reading to a young child, place him on your lap or put your arm around him. When he clears the dishes without your asking, give him a wink to show your appreciation. When he fails or makes a mistake, accept him as the imperfect person he must be—someone who does the best he can, a mixture of successes and failures;

not a perfect machine but a living, growing child. With tender loving care, your child, whoever he is, will continue to grow, to learn, to try because of your loving acceptance of him—each step of the way.

Parent and Teacher Working Together

The parents' best ally in helping the child be successful in school is the child's teacher. Go to school and visit your child's teacher. Let her know that you are interested in your child's schooling experience and ask for advice and direction in helping your child at home. Ask for information concerning your child's reading level, his math skills, and his demeanor in the classroom, and maintain a close communication with her throughout the school year. If you are having a problem with your child at home, share it with her and perhaps she will be able to give you some helpful advice concerning the matter. Do not be afraid to let her know how much you care about your child. It will help her to care, too.

Motivating Your Child

Motivating one's child to want to learn is one of the best gifts any parent can give. Motivation takes place through the child's observation of parent behavior and from listening to the words of the parent.

By reading themselves and by being interested in learning for its own sake, parents will motivate their children to want to imitate them and thus become avid learners also.

So What if He Doesn't Become the President of the United States?

We can't all become tops in the field, whatever that field may be. We can't all be the life of the party, the most interesting individual, the best cook, the strongest competitor, the fastest worker, the salesman with the best record, or the baby with the cutest dimples. Life doesn't work that way.

Perhaps your child isn't the best in his class or the most dynamic or the most interesting. Perhaps your child hates school and hates learning and seems to have no other interest than collecting frogs. If collecting frogs is what makes him happy, if he doesn't want to be the president of the United States, let him do his thing. He's involved, he's learning. He's growing, and at the same time he's being himself. As long as he fulfills the requirements of school and family responsibilities and is not harming himself or others, let him be what he wants to be and let him do what makes him happy. For children as well as for adults, success and happiness go hand in hand.

3

This Book: You and Your Child

The following chapters, which comprise the manual section of this book, have been written with two purposes in mind. The first is to inform the parents of an elementary school child what he is learning in school in the curriculum areas of language arts, math, social studies, and science. The second purpose is to provide activities for parents to use with their child and to give them ideas they can direct him toward that will reinforce his school learning. Because television is such a major influence on the children of our society, a special, final chapter has been included with the purpose of explaining to parents how they can use this medium as a learning experience for their child.

One of the problems encountered in summarizing the objectives of the school curriculum is that each school district has a different orientation to the teaching of the various curriculum areas. The specific orientations are based on the philosophical approach of each school district as well as the laws of each state concerning subject matter to be taught.

The similarities, however, far outweigh the differences. One school might teach American history at the fourth-grade level and another might teach it at the fifth- or sixth-grade level. But all children receive practically the same content throughout their elementary school years. Read the subject area summaries with this in mind. Just because your child is in the third grade does not necessarily mean that he will be introduced to everything that is explained in the third-grade math section. Indeed, he might very well be introduced to much more than my summary provides. These grade summaries have been formulated from curriculum guides and textbooks used throughout the United States. You can find out exactly what your child is learning in the various curriculum areas by speaking with your child, speaking with his teacher, or by looking through his textbooks and notebooks. From these three sources any parent can derive a complete understanding of what the child is learning for each subject area.

The activities I have provided for each of the four major learning areas that children are introduced to in the school are in no way meant to take the place of school lessons and the work that children are responsible for. Rather, they are meant to reinforce the school lessons in ways that are fun and entertaining and that hopefully make the child excited about and interested in learning. Their purpose is to enable children to see learning everywhere—not only in school but in the home, outdoors, or in front of a television set.

When you are looking for activities to enjoy with your child, please be aware that many of the activities listed for older children can be used with younger children as well, and vice versa. Flexibility is the key to the successful use of this book. Most of the activities for a specific area include experiences that will help your child in other subject areas as well. As children read guidebooks in preparation for a science trip in the woods, they are learning concepts that are often also included in the social studies area, as well as acquiring information that is based on knowledge of language arts and math.

A considerable variety of activities have been included for each subject area in order to give parents the opportunity to choose activities that the child enjoys doing. Some children may prefer the dice and card games from the math section, whereas others who have a natural ability in drawing may be more interested in doing the math activities that involve cutting, pasting, and working with geometric patterns. The main criterion that parents can use in picking and choosing activities is that the child is interested in them. Projects should present a challenge to a child without being too difficult for him. Most of all, the child should enjoy his work and should eagerly look forward to more.

Most of the activities are described in step-by-step instructions in order to make them as easy and as useful to the child as possible, without impinging upon the parents' daily schedules. Although they were designed for parents and children to do together, most of them can be incorporated into the child's interaction with his friends or older brothers and sisters. Many can be done by the child himself.

An attempt has been made to be as specific as possible in explaining the activities to parents. However, the descriptions are really meant to help parents use their own imagination; parents can use the activities as stepping stones to other activities that the child is interested in.

Each section contains tips and recommendations for working with your child. To get the most out of this book, read quickly through all the sections, check off the activities that you think will be of most interest to your child, and then go back to those particular activities when time permits.

Again, parent-child activities should have enjoyment as their basic criterion. When the child is enjoying the activity, learning will occur naturally. When parent and child are involved in activities that are enjoyable to both, the bonds of communication, commitment, love, and respect will be strengthened and deepened. Don't work with your child when you don't feel like it. Don't force your child to work with you when he is not interested. Don't put off other responsibilities you have in order to work with your child. Quality of time is the important factor in parent-child interaction, not quantity of time. Enjoying children and having them enjoy us is what parent-child relationships are all about.

Perhaps a more accurate title for this book would have been *Successful Parents*. The basic and overriding influence on any child's experience is the interaction between parent and child. Parents who love their children, who want to help their children do the very best they can, who take an interest in the lives of their children, and who are concerned about their welfare and do everything they can to help them succeed are successful parents. And successful parents produce successful children.

4

Language
Arts

The Five Major Objectives

Language arts is the most important curriculum area the child experiences in school learning. Through his study of language arts, the child acquires the specific language skills of reading, writing, speaking, listening, and such mechanics of communication as spelling, grammar, and punctuation. Without these skills learning in all other subject areas cannot proceed. The five major objectives of the language arts curriculum area are:

To teach children to communicate with maximum effectiveness in situations involving the organization, assimilation, and expression of ideas

To teach children how to read and to acquaint them with worthwhile literature; to help them enjoy reading and derive from literature an increased understanding of human behavior, ideals, and values; and to teach them how to use literature to find information and solve problems

To teach children how to think critically concerning their experiences with the mass media — in other words, to teach them discriminating and effective use of the media

To stimulate in children an interest in the study of language and to extend their appreciation of it as a learning tool and a medium of communication

To help children acquire self-confidence in their use of language in a variety of situations

The child begins to acquire skills in these areas during the first months of life, and no manual could even begin to explain all the variables that influence the learning of language. The activities presented in this section should be used as preliminary steps in helping the elementary school child develop language skills. Parents should consult with their children's school to discover additional helpful activities for their child.

Reading and Listening

Library

Join the neighborhood library and visit it regularly. Introduce yourself and your child to the librarian. Librarians are more than willing to help you choose books of particular interest, and they will keep you informed of library events and recommend the best books for your child. Take your child to the library for the weekly story hour and take advantage of the many other activities commonly offered by modern libraries, such as films, displays, special demonstrations, and after-school programs.

Helping Your Child Choose Books

Ages 0—3: Pre-school children are attracted to brightly colored books containing mostly pictures. They enjoy books that have a toylike quality: books with textures they can feel or a component that will pop out when manipulated in a certain way.

Ages 4—6: Nursery school and kindergarten children enjoy listening to simple fairy tales and nursery rhymes; picture story books that explain basic concepts are also popular at this age.

Ages 6—8: Early school-age children who are reading independently should be helped to choose books at their ability level. One good technique is to have the child open the book to a page somewhere in the middle and "try it out for size." If it can be read with relative ease, the child will probably enjoy that book. Keep in mind that books read for recreation should be slightly easier than the books used in school for instruction.

There are many publications available that can help parents choose children's books. The local library usually has these, but you can also order them through the mail. Some of these booklets are listed here.

Let's Read Together. Books for Family Enjoyment edited by the National Congress of Parents and Teachers and Children's Services Division, American Library Association. This bibliography contains over seven hundred titles grouped by reader interest and age level for children between two and fifteen years of age. To order, write: American Library Association, 50 East Huron Street, Chicago, Illinois 60611.

Bibliography of Books for Children An annotated bibliography of over fifteen hundred books for ages two to twelve. To order, write: Association for Childhood Education International, 3615 Wisconsin Avenue, N.W., Washington, D.C. 20016.

The Black Experience in Children's Books An annotated bibliography of 126 pages that is arranged by age group and subject matter in various geographical areas. To order, write: Office of Branch Library, New York Public Library, 8 East 40th Street, New York, New York 10016.

Caldecott Medal Books This is a list of award-winning picture books since 1938. To order, write: American Library Association, 50 East Huron Street, Chicago, Illinois 60611.

NOTE: These pamphlets range in cost from twenty cents to three dollars. Because the prices are subject to change, they are not included. Parents can ask the librarian or write the organization for information concerning cost and postage.

Reading Stories to Your Child

Reading aloud to children is one of the best ways parents can help children be successful in reading. In addition to books, newspapers and magazines are valuable reading materials for parents and children to share. *National Geographic* and *Reader's Digest* are two of the very best magazines for adults that children and parents can read together. Some of the best children's magazines are

Humpty Dumpty   This magazine, published monthly except during July and August, is good for children between the ages of four and six. It contains a wide assortment of games, activities, songs, puzzles, and poems that will reward your child with many hours of enjoyable learning.

Jack and Jill   This magazine for children between the ages of five and nine contains crossword puzzles, stories, cartoons, number games, lunch and dinner recipes, and seasonal activities that can be fun for both children and adults.

Children's Digest   An exciting magazine for children between the ages of eight and twelve years old that contains stories and activities that are full of fun and adventure.

Cricket   This wonderful magazine for children between the ages of six and twelve years old is specifically geared to help children acquire good reading habits. *Cricket* contains both fiction and nonfiction written by prize-winning authors, as well as poems, craft projects, puzzles, riddles, word games, and jokes, with lively illustrations throughout.

Highlights for Children   This magazine contains reading material for all elementary levels, with a wide variety of subject areas that include literature, social studies, science, as well as games, word fun, and party and craft ideas.

All of these magazines can be obtained at your local children's library and at most large newspaper and magazine stands.

Books, magazines, and newspapers can be used for a number of activities:

Vocabulary: Discuss unfamiliar words with your child. Look them up in the dictionary and use them in sentences.

Colors: Point out various colors to your child and have him point to different colors for you.

Size: Ask questions such as: "Where is the tallest giraffe?", "Find the little mouse.", "Put your finger on the big elephant."

Numbers: Questions to increase your child's awareness of numbers might include: "Let's count the cars.", "Where is the third bird?"

Discussion: Ask leading questions that will open a discussion, such as: "What would you have done if you had been ___?", "How do you think ____ felt in the story?", "What did you like best about this story?"

The great value of all reading experiences between parent and child is that they are shared activities. Reading should first and foremost be enjoyable and entertaining. The teaching-learning elements are secondary, for if the child enjoys the experience, learning will occur naturally. Remember, conversation during and after the story helps in the development of vocabulary and communication skills. Also keep in mind that mood and setting are important.

Find a quiet area in the home. Eliminate any distractions such as TV or radio. Sit close to your child or let him sit on your lap, making sure that he is comfortable. Let your child hold the book if possible or hold the book in front of him so that he can see it without difficulty.

Don't force your child to read with you. Rather, establish a regular routine at a time convenient for you both. If the child starts discussing some other topic that interests him, let him proceed. Then gradually try bringing him back to the story, or else continue the reading at another time.

Story-Time Activities for Preschool, Kindergarten, and First-Grade Children

1. Have your child make a simple picture booklet of the story by having him draw his own pictures to portray events in the story.

2. Have your child retell the story to another family member in his own words.

3. Have your child act out the parts of the characters as the story is being reread.

4. Make masks of various characters in the story out of paper bags, drawing and coloring faces on them and cutting holes for the eyes, nose, and mouth.

5. On individual cards or pieces of paper draw simple pictures depicting the events of the story. Shuffle the cards. The child turns over one card at a time and must put them in the proper sequential order of the story. This activity can be done with any number of cards, depending on the age and maturity of the child.

6. Reread the story leaving out key words and have your child supply them.

EXAMPLE: "Once upon a time there were three ____."
"The first one built his house out of ____."

7. Retell the story, having your child add a new ending to it.

8. After reading a story, pick an object or thing from the story and play the "If I Were . . ." game. The parent says, "If I were a tree . . .," and the child continues by stating various characteristics of the object.

> EXAMPLE: "If I were a tree, I would have brown bark and green leaves, and I would live in the forest."
>
> Encourage your child to think of all the consequences, such as:
>
> "Birds would live in my branches"; "my leaves would turn brown in the fall"; "maybe I would be cut down and made into paper."

9. Have your child tell you his own story. Write it down for him and hang it someplace where the entire family can read and praise it. Encourage him to draw a picture to go with it.

10. Make simple hand puppets out of small paper bags or fabric and have your child make up his own stories.

To make paper-bag puppets: Color the faces on the bag and cut out holes for fingers to be used as puppet arms.

To make fabric puppets: Sew fabric into a mitten shape to cover hand; sew on buttons or different colored fabric to make the face.

Readiness Activities for Prereaders

Before children can read, they must first develop certain essential abilities called readiness skills. Such experiences can begin when your child is two and three years old. By answering his many questions, engaging him in conversation, and by reading to him, parents help the child develop his language abilities. Through these parent-child encounters children develop skill in vocabulary, speech, and listening. Children who can listen effectively, who have a good working vocabulary, and who can express themselves well have an advantage when it comes to learning to read.

When children are four and five years old, they are usually ready for more formal reading readiness activities. Such experiences can include practice in vocabulary development, listening skills and concentration, visual and auditory discrimination, story sequence and left to right eye movement—all necessary skills for reading. The following activities for prereaders that focus on specific aspects of reading readiness are, for the most part, for children who are four and five years old.

But before continuing, a word of caution must be expressed. Parents should not force children to engage in any of these activities. These experiences should be enjoyable for both child and parent, and no pressure should be placed on the child because this may frustrate him or turn him off to reading.

Learning should stem from the child's natural curiosity, not from force. You can motivate your child to want to learn to read by providing stimulating books for him, by reading to him, by taking him to the library, by being a reader yourself, and most of all by showing him how pleased you are that he is interested in reading.

VOCABULARY DEVELOPMENT

1. Have your child make scrapbooks by cutting pictures out of magazines and pasting them on paper to make a car book, a boat book, a clothing book, an animal book, a people book, and so forth. Label each picture with its appropriate word.

2. Help your child compile his own alphabet book. Pick a subject such as animals. Have him cut pictures of animals out of magazines, old books, newspapers, and catalogues. Mount a picture for each letter on a separate piece of paper and label it with its letter and word (*A-ant; B-bee; C-cat; D-dog;* etc.) Then staple the pages together.

3. Post the child's name in significant places such as over the place for his towel in the bathroom or in his own books. (Remember to write in print.)

4. Make an "All About Me" book. Use a snapshot of the child for the cover, with the title "All About Me" and the child's name. Inside, the child can draw pictures of various things he cares about. Choose from his home, pets, favorite toys, best friend, family, and so on. Each page may be labeled as dictated by the child.

5. Beginning readers enjoy cutting out words they know from magazines or newspaper headlines. These may be pasted onto colored paper and read aloud. Appropriate words may be illustrated.

AUDITORY DISCRIMINATION: INITIAL CONSONANTS AND RHYMING

1. Say two words and have your child tell whether they are the same word or two different words.

> EXAMPLES: *bug, bug*
> *bug, rug*
> *hat, mat*
> *hat, hat*

2. Say two words and have your child tell whether they begin with the same sound or are different.

> EXAMPLES: *boat, bone*
> *nickel, mommy*
> *table, take*
> *radio, television*

3. Say two words and have your child tell whether or not they rhyme.

> EXAMPLES: *time, dime*
> *look, cook*
> *ball, can*

LISTENING SKILLS AND CONCENTRATION

1. Parent and child close their eyes and listen to the different sounds in the house and on the street. Discuss what you hear.

2. Have your child identify the sound as you

crumple or tear a piece of paper
bounce a ball
scribble with a pencil
blow out air
stomp your feet
turn a light switch on and off
scratch material

3. Play the game "What Animal Am I?" The parent makes the sound of an animal, and the child has to guess what animal (or machine) it is.

4. Call out a series of names, letters, words, or numbers and have your child repeat them. Begin with a series of two or three and increase the amount as your child improves his skill.

> EXAMPLES: *1, 7, 9*
> *Jack, Mary, Nancy, Kay*

READING FROM LEFT TO RIGHT

1. "Where Is My Home?" Draw a picture of an animal on the left side of the page (bird, dog, horse) and another picture of where the animal lives on the right side of the page (bird's nest, doghouse, barn).

The child draws a line from the left side of the page to the home of the animal on the right side.

2. Place dots across the page and have your child draw lines with a pencil or crayon connecting them.

When Children Learn to Read

One good method of providing reinforcement for children who know how to read is to have them read aloud to the parent. Such exercises in oral reading allow the parent to assist the child with any difficult words, to help the child read with correct verbal expression and comprehension, and to praise the child for his achievement. Encourage your child to select books that he can read, and when he does not know a word, say it for him and let him continue reading without interruption. After he finishes the story, you can always go back and review the words that were missed. Have a dictionary nearby to look up the meaning of any difficult words and encourage him to use it without your help.

But just because your child is now reading on his own, do not stop reading stories to him. Children of all ages find immense satisfaction in having their parents read to them.

Activities for Children Who Can Read

CHILDREN'S CORNER   Use a corner of your living room or the child's bedroom for a collection of books, reference materials, and learning games. Adults have a space for reading and working, and so should children. A small rug and chair can provide your child with his own little "study."

LOCATING INFORMATION   Help your child acquire skills in locating information by providing opportunities for him to find words in the dictionary, names in the telephone book, types of businesses in the Yellow Pages, statistics in the almanac, and facts in encyclopedias. Start by doing these things together, then have your child find the information on his own.

LOCAL NEWS   Subscribe to local newspapers so that your child can read the local, national, and international news. Help him become aware of the different sections of the paper—news, financial, sports, advertising, editorials, weather, politics, comics, and so forth. Discuss articles of mutual interest.

REINFORCING VOCABULARY

1. From magazines and newspapers have your child cut out words that he is learning in school. Place them in a box and have him pick out words from the box and form sentences with them.

2. Encourage him to keep a file of new vocabulary words. Using three-by-five index cards, the child prints the word in large letters on one side of the card and writes the definition of the word on the other side of the card. (Younger children may find it easier to incorporate the word into a simple phrase rather than give a formal definition.) Keep the cards in a cigar box or envelope. Go over the words with him every so often, and as you do, have him say the word in a sentence.

3. From your child's reader or library books make a list of words that describe emotions and feeling situations and have him cut out magazine pictures that illustrate the words. Some words that can be used for this type of exercise are *love, anger, happiness, peace, lazy, shy, anxious, hopeful, disappointed, fearful, tired, scared, thoughtful, sorrow, joy.*

4. The game called "Ghost" is a lot of fun, and it gives reinforcement learning in spelling as well as vocabulary. One family member begins the game by calling out a letter. In turn, each participant calls out an additional letter to spell the beginning of a word. He tries to add his letter so as to cause one of the other players to complete a word by adding the final letter of a word. However, he must have a specific word in mind and if the combination of letters he is proposing is improbable, he may be challenged by another player. Any individual who ends a word gets a letter from the word *ghost.* The first person to spell the word *ghost* this way (that is, after losing five rounds of the game) is the loser.

Any player can challenge another player on his letter if it is thought that the letter added to the other letters does not spell a word correctly. When a person is challenged, he must tell the other players the word he had in mind. If it is a word, the person who challenged gets a letter in *ghost;* if it is not a properly spelled word, the person who called the letter gets one of the letters in *ghost.*

5. "Follow My Word" is a category game in which one player calls out a word in the chosen category, and then the next player, using the same category, must call out another word that begins with the last letter of the word called by the player before him.

EXAMPLE: If the category chosen is animals, the first player might call out the word *horse.* The next player must think of an animal word that begins with *e*, such as *elephant*. The next animal word would then have to begin with *t*, such as *tiger*. Other categories might be names of cities, first names, countries, rivers.

6. To play "The First Letter," choose any letter from the alphabet and add on additional letters from one to as many letters as can be added to form different words. The players must guess the word.

EXAMPLE: If the chosen letter is *b*, the first player says, "My word begins with *b* and has one other letter." The other players must guess the word *by*. The second player uses *b* with two additional letters, for example, *buy*. The next player must think of a word that begins with *b* and has three additional letters, for example, *bent*. The next word could be *bring*; then next, *become*; and so on, until a word with additional letters that begins with *b* cannot be found.

USING THE DICTIONARY

1. Children who are familiar with the dictionary can practice estimating the location of words in their alphabetical order. Call out a word and have the child open the dictionary to the approximate page on which the word might be located. Depending on the size of the dictionary being used, establish a limit on the number of pages, say five or twenty-five, between which you both consider a good estimate has been made of the location of the word.

2. One family member locates a word in the dictionary that is rarely used in everyday conversation. Words such as *cephalalgia*, *ovoviviparous*, and *zoolatry* are some examples. Each family member writes down what they think is the meaning of the word. Encourage your family to use their imagination and humor in writing their definitions. The definitions are read aloud, and then the dictionary is used to find the proper definition.

3. Have your child use his dictionary to locate words that, when spelled backward, form another word.

EXAMPLES: *pat*   *tap*
          pan   *nap*
          tub   *but*

He can also use the dictionary to locate words that are made up of two smaller words.

EXAMPLES: *some/where*
to/day
over/coat
air/plane

4. Discuss with your child vocabulary words that have multiple meanings, such as *glasses, run, duck, head, ring, bark, lie*. Have him look for other words that have multiple meanings in the dictionary.

COMPREHENSION   Comprehension is the most important aspect of reading. Any child who is lacking in this reading skill will probably be deficient in almost all subject areas. Whatever the subject, the child who cannot understand what he is reading will not be able to apply it to his life or growth.

The following activities can be used to reinforce your child's comprehension skills.

1. Have your child read a story and answer questions such as the following:

"What might three other titles for the story be?"

"What would you have done if you were in the story?"

"Who is the most important person in the story? Why do you think so?"

"What did you learn from the story?"

2. For comprehension practice in following instructions, have your child read and follow your instructions to locate "the prize."

EXAMPLE: "Begin at the bathroom door and take three steps into the hallway. Make a left turn and take five steps into the bedroom. Turn right, take one step, bend down, and you will find further directions for locating the prize."

3. Make up riddles for your child. Have him read them and then draw a picture of the answer. Have your child draw riddles for you to answer.

EXAMPLES: *Riddles for young children*
"It is a pet. It likes to eat and eat. It can go hop, hop, hop. What is it?"

"It is a new toy. It is red. It has a hose and ladder. What is it?"

EXAMPLES: *Riddles for older children*
"It has two wheels. It can go seventeen miles per hour. You can get one when you are sixteen years old. What is it?" (A moped.)

"First it lives in a tree or plant. Then it crawls on the ground. Then it flies in the air. What is it?" (A butterfly.)

4. Write paragraphs about different things and situations. Make up titles on separate pieces of paper and have your child select the appropriate title for each paragraph. Older children can cut out paragraphs from the newspaper, read them, and make up appropriate titles.

5. Write paragraphs including one sentence that does not belong in the paragraph. Have your child read the paragraph and cross out the sentence that does not belong.

EXAMPLE: *A paragraph for young children*
"The dog is black and brown. His name is Charlie. He likes to run and jump. Charlie is a beautiful dog. *It is a nice day.*"

EXAMPLE: *A paragraph for older children*
"The spacemen landed on the moon. They brought the right equipment to do experiments. Rock and dirt samples were collected. *The moon can be seen from the earth.* They brought the samples back to earth."

6. Complete the sentence with a picture. Give your child sentences that are incomplete and have him cut out a magazine picture that completes the sentence.

EXAMPLES: "Tommy and Chris were playing with ___." (The child might cut out a picture of a dog.)

"Theresa bought a new ___ for Christine." (doll, coat, car, etc.)

"They went to the ___." (beach, park, mountains, etc.)

This same exercise can be done by using words. Give your child sentences and have him underline the one word that best completes the sentence.

EXAMPLES: "The storm caused the ship to (fall, *sink*, break)."

"The girl ran a fast (*race*, walk, bicycle)."

"The radio was too (noisy, quick, *loud*)."

7. Have your child write sentences that go along with pictures that he has cut out from magazines. Mix them up and have him match the sentences with the pictures.

8. Scramble the words in a sentence and have your child rearrange the sentences so that they make sense.

> EXAMPLES: "The dog took Jim and Marilyn for a walk."
> "The passengers carried the boat to the other side of the river."

MEMORY, VISUAL PERCEPTION, AND LISTENING SKILLS

1. Show your child a number of objects such as a spoon, a pen, a ball, a book. Let him touch them and name them for you. Then hide the objects under a cloth or paper and have him repeat the names of the objects that he saw. This can be done with five to fifteen objects, depending on the child's development.

2. Give your child a number of directions to carry out after hearing them only once.

> EXAMPLES: *For young children*
>
> "Clap your hands, turn around, and jump up and down."
>
> "Bring me one shoe, two napkins, and three magazines."
>
> "Draw three triangles, five rectangles, and seven squares."

> EXAMPLES: *For older children*
>
> "Use this ruler to find the length, width, and height of the table."
>
> "Seventeen girls, fifteen boys, and ten adults went on a picnic. How many people attended the picnic?"
>
> "Find four aces, three kings, and two queens in this deck of cards."

3. To give your child practice in visual discrimination, make up work sheets consisting of groups of four pictures, with one of the pictures in each group a little different from the others. The child must circle the picture that is not like the others.

EXAMPLES: *For young children*

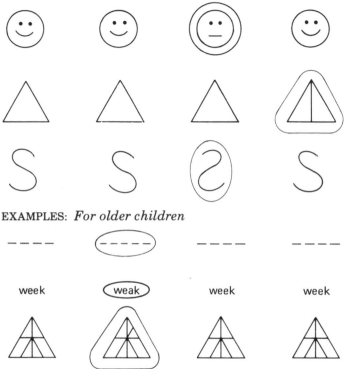

EXAMPLES: *For older children*

4. A good family game for practicing listening and memory skills is begun by one person who says: "I am going to the store to buy peaches." The next player repeats the sentence and adds an additional word or phrase, such as: "I am going to the store to buy peaches and bananas" or "I am going to the store to buy peaches and bananas for my Aunt Katie." Each player continues to add to the original phrase until one player forgets a word or phrase, at which time play begins again.

Reading Section Summary

These activities are only some of the things that parents can do with their children to reinforce reading in the home. They are meant to help the child progress in a happy and healthy manner. Their purpose is not to take the place of the child's schooling experience in any way whatsoever but rather to help the child gain as much as possible from that experience. Besides these activities, parents can avail themselves of the following opportunities:

1. Initiate a close communication with your child's teacher. Inform her of your desire to work with your child in the home, of your interest in the child's school progress, and of your appreciation for the role she is playing in your child's life.

2. Introduce yourself to the principal of the school. Let him know of your desire to work with him and his teachers in the education of your child.

3. Join the parents' association to keep yourself informed of school policy and school programs.

4. Find out what reading program is being used in your child's school, the philosophy of the program, and the number of hours each day your child spends on reading.

5. Acquire more information from books that have been written on the subject of how you can help your child in reading (see Bibliography).

Handwriting

Manuscript

Handwriting is not easy for many children. This skill that we adults take for granted as a part of our daily experience is an acquired skill that combines a truly intricate interplay of the mind and the body. It takes considerable practice to develop the necessary muscle control, eye-hand coordination, and memory skills for proper writing. In helping the child develop this skill, the parent should realize that although certain children have a natural ability for good writing, others do not, and that "good" or "poor" writing ability is no indicator of intelligence. The important thing is to help your child do his best while not pushing him too much.

Readiness practice in handwriting can begin when your child is three years old. The ability to write requires control of eye, hand, and arm. Activities that give children experience in coordinating their eye and hand movements are

putting puzzles together
cutting with scissors
tracing with pencil over lines and figures
zippering and buttoning clothes
hammering nails

catching balls
stringing beads
brush and finger painting
crayon coloring
scribbling

To give your child readiness practice in writing on the line, simply draw a few lines across a page and have your child draw pictures of people, flowers, balls, houses, and so on, so that the objects are "standing" on the line.

To give your child practice in the basic strokes of manuscript writing, have him draw circles and lines and then combine them to make various objects.

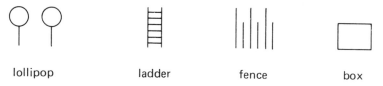

EXAMPLES: "Let's make a ball."

"Let's make a stick standing up."

"Let's make a stick lying down."

"Let's make a slide."

"Let's make a slide going the other way."

Children can combine the strokes to make various objects, using unlined paper.

lollipop   ladder   fence   box

GETTING STARTED   Children in kindergarten and first grade begin by learning to write their names and other familiar words. They are taught to follow certain rules:

All letters must rest on the line.

The spacing between letters must be neither too wide nor too narrow.

Raise the pencil after each stroke.

Begin writing all letters from the top.

Make all letters and numbers with straight lines and circles (*N*, *O*, *L*, *i*) or parts of circles (*D*, *C*, *p*).

Vertical and horizontal strokes

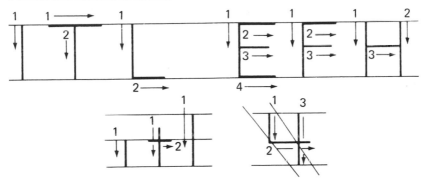

Counter clockwise strokes

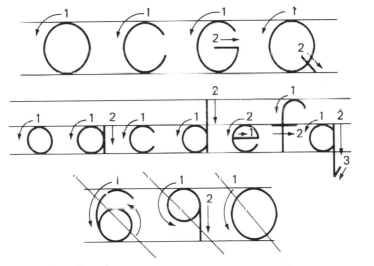

Vertical and slanted strokes

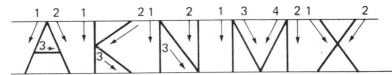

Some letters are made with vertical and horizontal strokes, some with vertical and slanted strokes and others with counterclockwise or clockwise strokes.

Vertical and slanted strokes

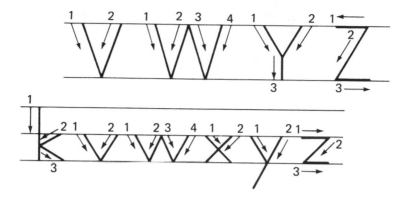

Clockwise strokes

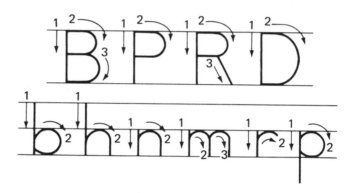

Clockwise and counter-clockwise strokes

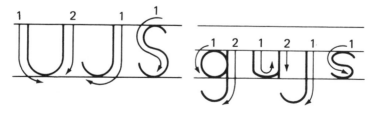

Good writing requires correct positioning. The child should face the table or desk squarely while resting both arms upon it. Have him sit in an erect position, well back in his seat, with both feet resting comfortably upon the floor. The lower edge of the paper should be parallel to the edge of the table.

There are different models that schools select to use as guides for children learning to print. These variations in letter structure (K, K, K, K) are used throughout America, and the parent can become familiar with his child's school's particular style by looking at the child's workbook or talking to the teacher.

MANUSCRIPT ACTIVITIES

1. The first thing a child will want to write is his name. Show him the letter forms and have him write his name, disregarding the standard norms of size until he is comfortable with the letters. You can tape his work to the objects he uses in the home, such as his chair, his toy box, his bureau, and so on.

2. Have your child write a letter to grandmother, a favorite uncle, aunt, or cousin. He can draw a picture on the front of a folded piece of paper and, with the parent's help, write a few lines on the inside, such as:

> Dear Grandmother,
> Here is a picture of our house. I love you.
> > Tommy

Grandmother will be thrilled!

3. Using dry cereal in the shape of the letters of the alphabet, have your child pick out one letter at a time and then write that letter on a piece of paper. When he has finished, he can place the cereal letters in alphabetical order.

4. Using the dictionary, have your child copy the longest word he can find that begins with the letter T (use any letter), the smallest word that begins with the letter Y, three words that begin with W, and write down words that have three i's in them, or two p's or four s's.

SCRIPT (CURSIVE)   In the middle grades (grades 2, 3 and 4) children are taught how to write in script. Right-handed children should tilt their paper to the left at an angle of about 30 degrees. The left-handed writer should tilt the paper to the right at about the same angle. The child should hold his paper with the hand that he is not using to write with.

In making the transition from print to script, children are taught that some letter forms are different in script than they are in print, that script letters are slanted, and that the letters are joined.

The first letters learned are those that are similar in the two types of writing: i, *i* ; d, *d* ; w, *w* ; and so on. Then the children receive instruction in the letters that are different in the two forms: b, *b* ; f, *f* ; s, *s* ; and so on.

Every so often a child will have particular difficulty with one or two letters of the alphabet. If this occurs, have your child make the letter on paper without lines, disregarding the standard letter size. After he becomes comfortable with the letter, have him practice it on lined paper by writing the letter by itself and then writing words that contain the letter.

Don't push your child in his writing abilities. Let him progress at his own pace. Give him ideas that combine practice in writing with composition exercises such as:

writing letters to family, politicians, famous individuals, various organizations and societies

writing book reports

writing the shopping list

keeping a diary

writing short stories

Creative Expression

Poetry

Poetry is one of the most universal and powerful means of creative expression. Anyone and everyone can participate in this type of experience. In addition to helping children learn vocabulary and increase their ability to use words in various ways, poetry shows children the beauty of language and enables them to express their feelings in a creative manner.

Poems appropriate to the seasons, holidays, and national and international events are entertaining for children of all ages. *Skip Around the Year*, by Aileen Fisher (Crowell, 1967), and *More Poetry for Holidays*, selected by Nancy Larrick (Garrard, 1973), are good anthologies. *Poems and Verses to Begin On*, edited by Donald Bissett (Noble and Noble, 1967), and Bissett's other book, *Poems and Verses About Animals* (Noble and Noble, 1967), are especially good for urban children.

And don't forget the two wonderful books by Kenneth Koch concerning poetry for children. His first book, *Wishes, Lies, and Dreams: Teaching Children to Write Poetry* (Chelsea House, 1970) is an anthology of poems by the students of P.S. 61 in Manhattan and gives a great variety of ideas for motivating children to write poetry. The second is called *Rose, Where Did You Get That Red? Teaching Poetry to Children* (Random House, 1973). It describes his method of teaching poems to children and is a marvelous combination of handbook, anthology, and instructor's guide.

POETRY RECITALS   These recitals can provide an evening of entertainment for the entire family and friends. Everyone sits around in a circle and each individual reads a few poems to the group and maybe even recites his own poetry. Recitations are good for children of all ages. Young children can recite rhymes, such as:

> Rain, rain, go away,
> Come again some other day,
> Little [child's name] wants to play.

> Starlight, star bright,
> First star I've seen tonight,
> I wish I may, I wish I might,
> Have the wish I wish tonight.

Older children can recite poems, fables, or a story they are reading in school. Recitations should be a family affair. Children like to imitate the actions of their parents, so parents should recite first to show their children how it is done and to motivate them to perform also.

POETRY WRITING   Encourage your child to create his own poetry. It's not as difficult as it might sound and can be a lot of fun.

POETRY ACTIVITIES
For young children

1. Give your child any line of your own and have him complete it with a line of his own.

> EXAMPLES: Parent: "Once in a while . . ."
> Child: "I walk a mile."
>
> Parent: "My Aunt Sadie . . ."
> Child: "Is a very nice lady."
>
> Parent: "In the house . . ."
> Child: "I saw a mouse."

2. As you read poems to your child, have him pantomime what they say.

> EXAMPLE: "I'm a little teapot tall and stout,
> This is my handle, this is my spout,
> Just tip me over and pour me out."

As you read, the child places one hand on his hip so that his arm juts out like a handle, extends the other as a spout, and bends to the side to simulate pouring.

3. Call out words and have your child think of another word that rhymes with yours.

EXAMPLES: *play*   *may*   *say*
           fly   *high*   *sky*
           car   *star*   *far*

For older children

1. Encourage your child to start his own special book of poems. In it he can transcribe poems he likes and write poems of his own creation.

2. Keep a family book of poetry in which each family member records his or her own poetry, or again, transcribes favorites from other books.

3. Attend poetry readings at the local college or cultural center. Consult your local newspaper or your town information service for dates and times.

POETRY BOOKS   Poems and rhymes are a beautiful medium for the development of vocabulary and word usage. The following books on rhymes and poems are good.

For beginning readers

Mother Goose Nursery Rhymes, selected by Arthur Rackham (Viking, 1975), is a collection of verses complete with drawings and decorations that provide a great deal of enjoyment for children and parents.

Songs the Sandman Sings, compiled by Gwendolyn Reed, with drawings by Peggy Skillen (Atheneum, 1969), is an illustrated collection of English and American poetry specially selected for reading at bedtime. This book is especially good for prekindergarten and kindergarten levels.

The Oxford Book of Children's Verse, edited by Iona and Archibald Opie (Oxford University, 1973), is an entertaining collection of classic British and American poetry.

For grades 2–3

Listen, Children, Listen; An Anthology of Poems for the Very Young, edited by Myra Livingston, with illustrations by Trina

Hyman (Harcourt, Brace & Jovanovich, 1972), is an anthology that explores the world of children through poetry accompanied by whimsical drawings.

Catch Your Breath: A Book of Shivery Poems, selected by Lilian Moore and Lawrence Webster, with illustrations by Gahan Wilson (Garrard, 1973), is a collection of poems that depicts howling winds and stormy seas, witches and scary scenes.

For grades 4–6

The Golden Book of Fun and Nonsense, edited by Louis Untermeyer, with illustrations by Alice and Martin Provensen (Golden Press, 1970), is an illustrated collection of nursery rhymes and nonsense poetry by Ogden Nash, Lewis Carroll, T. S. Eliot, and other poets whose work will delight both children and adults.

Poems of Lewis Carroll, selected by Myra Livingston, with illustrations by John Tenniel, Harry Furniss, Henry Holiday, Arthur Frost, and Lewis Carroll, from the original editions (Crowell, 1973), is a collection of poems from *Alice's Adventures in Wonderland*, *Through the Looking Glass*, and *What Alice Found Out There*, in addition to other humorous verse, puzzles, and riddles.

Songs

Songs, like poetry, are a wonderful way of learning vocabulary and interacting with others easily and naturally. Endless in number, anyone and everyone can find songs they like and can share them with the other family members. Some good songbooks follow:

For grades Pre-K–3

Songs to Sing to the Very Young, compiled by Phyllis Ohanian, with illustrations by Marjorie Torrey (Random House, 1966), is a book of songs of melodic tunes accompanied by delightful pictures. Children will enjoy singing "Mary Had a Little Lamb," "Hickory Dickory Dock," "Sing a Song of Sixpence," and many other favorites.

The Sesame Street Songbook, with words and music by Joe Raposo and Jeffrey Moss, arrangements by Sy Oliver, illustrated by Loretta Trezzo (Simon and Schuster, 1971), presents the music and lyrics to thirty-six songs from the popular children's television show, including "Bein' Green" and "Rubber Duckie."

The Wheels on the Bus Go Round and Round, compiled by Nancy Larrick, illustrated by Gene Holtan, with music arrangements by Patty Zeitlin (Golden Gate Junior Books, 1972), contains delightful drawings and verse that illustrate an array of songs designed to entertain youngsters who travel to school on buses.

For grades 4–6

The Fireside Book of Children's Songs, edited by Marie Winn, illustrated by John Alcorn, music arranged by Allan Miller (Simon and Schuster, 1966), is a collection of the words and music for many international songs, including bedtime, animal, and nursery songs.

The Gambit Book of Children's Songs, compiled by Donald Mitchell and Roderick Bliss, with illustrations by Errol Le Cain (Gambit, 1970), offers Western folk songs illustrated with line drawings.

Songs of '76: A Folksinger's History of the Revolution, compiled by Oscar Brand (Evans, 1972), is a collection of songs sung during the American Revolution accompanied by explanatory notes revealing the ideas and attitudes of the colonists and British soldiers.

Stories and Composition

DIARY Encourage your child to keep a diary of the meaningful events of the day or the week as well as the child's personal feelings about them. This can be expanded into an album by including photographs, mementoes of places visited, letters and postcards received, report cards and schoolwork, favorite poems, dreams, and thoughts about the future.

PICTURES Give your child an interesting picture and have him tell or write a story following the outline below:

What is happening in the picture?

What probably happened before this scene took place?

What may happen next?

What are the characters doing and saying?

What would you do if you were in this picture?

Make up a serious, funny, or sad conversation between the characters in the picture.

IMAGINARY STORIES   Try presenting ideas such as the following to help motivate your child to write a story:

> "You are the first person to land on Venus. Write a story concerning your trip and what Venus is like."

> "You have been elected mayor of our town. What would you do to make life better for the citizens?"

> "You and a friend find yourselves shipwrecked in the middle of the Atlantic Ocean with only a small raft and a box of dried food. Write a story about your adventures."

NEW ENDINGS   Use stories from the child's reader as well as fairy tales and library books and have him create his own original endings to the story. Ask him to make up a happy ending and a sad ending for the same story.

TITLES AND HEADLINES   Give your child paragraphs from magazine and newspaper stories—both fiction and nonfiction—and have him make up titles or headlines concerning the paragraph.

Family Activities

Family activities are filled with potential language arts learning experiences. Such family-oriented activities can reinforce the child's school learning in an informal and entertaining way.

Dinner Table Conversation

Anywhere and anyplace the parent and child are, conversation can serve as a learning experience as well as a source for bonds of love and affection. Conversation also develops verbal skills and instills habits of discussion and inquiry. For many families dinnertime has proved to be the best time of the day to talk to one another. But whatever time your family finds most convenient, be it in the car, on a walk, or in the living room, remember that conversation is one of the most, if not the most, important factors in a child's language development.

Conversation between parents and children is not often easy to come by. Parents must play the role of disciplinarian and advisor as well as conversationalist, and at certain times it is difficult to separate these roles. Here are some guidelines for starting conversations with children and for keeping them going:

Choose a topic that is of interest to you as well as to the child.

Keep the conversation on a light, friendly basis; deemphasize both the teacher-student learning relationship and the parent-child advisor relationship.

Explore all aspects of the topic, such as amount, size, time, when, where, how, why.

Theorize by using imaginative questions such as "What if . . .?" "Could you imagine . . .?"

Play games that begin with questions such as: "If you could be anybody in the world, who would you be?" or "If you could live in any period of history, what period would you choose?"

When your child asks a question, praise him once in a while before giving the answer to impress upon him the importance of asking questions: "That is a very smart question; you are a bright child to want to know these things."

When your child asks a question to which you do not know or are not sure of the answer, tell him where he can find the answer: "We can look in the encyclopedia (dictionary, almanac, atlas) for the answer", or "We can go to the library and find a book on that subject."

Ask your child questions when it seems that something is bothering him. Get him used to the idea of expressing problems and finding comfort through communication. If your child finds it difficult to express negative feelings to you, try the following technique: "Wow, did I have a bad day today. Let me tell you about it. I always feel better after I talk about the things that are bothering me." (Parent tells highlights of the bad day to the child.) "Is anything bothering you? You can tell me about it if you like."

It doesn't really matter what a parent and child talk about so long as they are communicating and exploring ideas and feelings in a lively way. But sometimes a little planning helps get the conversational ball rolling.

A great technique for initiating dinner table conversation that was used by the Kennedy family—see *A Time to Remember* by Rose Kennedy (Doubleday, 1974)—is to pick a topic in the morning and post it where every family member can see it and think about it during the day. That evening everyone in the family contributes his or her thoughts in a discussion far more likely to be lively than on a topic thought up at the last minute. The discussion should take into consideration the level of understanding of each child, but almost all discussion topics can be explained in simplified ways so that a child of almost any age can understand. Some topics for young children might be

1. When I grow up, what can I be? Begin with professions that your child knows about, such as that of teacher, doctor, dentist, policeman, fireman, and so on. Have your child explain what a doctor does, for example, and then talk to him about the ramifications of the field of medicine, the necessary preparation for becoming a doctor, and the advantages and disadvantages of the medical profession.

2. How is information communicated in our world? Discuss schools of various levels (high school, college, vocational) and the various news media, such as newspapers, television, radio, magazines, books, films.

3. How is the world different now from the way it was a hundred years ago, fifty years ago, twenty years ago? Talk about the telephone, TV, radio, cars, planes, satellites, electricity, housing, industries, and different life-styles. How have these things improved living conditions throughout the world? How has our neighborhood changed because of these things?

Some topics for older children might be:

1. Who do you think should be the next president (mayor) of our country (city)? Talk about the politicians running for elective office, their personalities, their platforms, their records, the two-party system in the United States, the roles of minority parties in American politics. Who were the great politicians? Why and how did "Watergate" come about? How can our system of government be improved? Compare our system of government with communism, dictatorships, socialistic countries and how our system of government is the best.

2. Why do human beings do the things we do? Why do we work, eat,

sleep, play, love, hate, and die? What is the role of work and play in life?

3. How did the sports boom in America come about? Why are sports a healthy form of entertainment? What is the difference between playing tennis and watching a tennis match on television?

4. What role can art play in the lives of people? What is an artist? How does art give people enjoyment? Where can we go for artistic recreation? How does art influence advertising, architecture, consumer products? What role did religion play in the evolution of art? Who are the great artists throughout history? What is your favorite art form?

5. If you could live in any historical period, which one would you choose? The colonial period in America? The Renaissance in Europe? How did people dress during these periods? What type of work did they do? What were living conditions like? How is life different today?

Families might also consider listening to the radio or TV news before or during the first part of dinner and then discussing the events of the day. In addition to giving children practice in listening and communicating about current events, it also enriches the dinner hour and provides endless topics of conversation (see chapter 8).

Family Hour

The idea behind family hour is obvious enough: One hour every evening everyone in the family sits down together to talk, to read, to work, to play a game, or to make something together. Conversation revolving around family activities such as these has the same benefit for children's verbal development and for developing bonds of love and affection within the family as dinnertime conversation. Activities the whole family can participate in, such as making collections, playing games, and singing songs, provide children with experiences in social interaction, as well as language development and knowledge acquisition.

MAKING COLLECTIONS   Seeds, shells, coins, stamps, rocks, leaves, pressed wildflowers are all possible objects to collect. There are books and magazines available on almost any kind of collectible you desire. For children ages eight and up, *Charlie Brown's Super Book of Things to Do and Collect*, written and illustrated by Charles Schulz (Random House, 1975), is ideal. Charlie Brown and his gang show how to collect stamps, rocks, leaves, fingerprints, and many other objects. *The Family Book of Hobbies*, by the editors of Sterling (Sterling, 1973), contains descriptions of native collecting as well as creative, outdoor, and performing hobbies for older children and parents to enjoy. See Bibliography for additional listings.

CRAFTS   Embroidery, crochet, needlepoint, knitting, rug hooking, loom weaving, macrame, and candle making are just a few of the special-equipment crafts a family can enjoy. *A Beginner's Book of Patchwork, Appliqué, and Quilting*, by Constance Bogen (Dodd, Mead, 1974), gives instructions for turning pieces of fabric into patchwork, appliqué, and quilts, along with suggestions for various projects. *The Tall Book of Candle Crafting*, by Gary Guy, with photos by Dave Pedegana (Sterling, 1974), gives instructions for making simple and intricate candle creations, with discussions on colors and waxes.

A list of other craft books specifically for children follows:

Toy Book, by Steven Caney (Workman, 1972), is a lovely book that tells how to make discovery toys, pretending toys, games, building toys, action toys, and design toys from materials often found around the house. All of them work, and all have been tested by children in play situations.

Beginning Crafts for Beginning Readers, by Alice Gilbreath (Follett, 1972), is particularly good for beginning readers, but fine for younger children with parental help and for older children too. Engaging, easy-to-make toys from ordinary materials—a plastic-lid raft, an egg-carton caterpillar, a spool totem pole, and so on.

What Can I Do Today? A Treasure of Crafts for Children, by Joan Klimo (Pantheon, 1971), contains large, bright, full-color illustrations and step-by-step directions illustrated with drawings for unusually clear and engaging projects, including Magic Starchies, Crazy Pasta, Giant Carrot Pencil Holder, Moon City. Includes instructions for several kinds of collages.

Children's Crafts, by the editors of Sunset Books (Sunset Books, 1976), presents a wide variety of entertaining activities, craft items, games, and playthings that can be made with paper, cloth, found objects, natural objects, foods, and other materials.

Treasury of Creative Handcraft Activities for Elementary Teachers, by Louise Arangis (Parker, 1976). This useful book for parents as well as teachers describes projects that can be adapted to different age groups and includes activities for handicapped children.

The Little Kid's Americana Craft Book, by Jackie Vermeer (Taplinger, 1975), gives clear instructions for making those things that children constructed seventy-five years ago, such as paper dolls, homemade games, and outdoor toys.

Shopping Craft Art, by James Seidelman and Grace Mintoyne (Crowell-Collier, 1970), suggests ways to make a great variety of projects, including paper-bag puppets, vegetable prints, walk-through sculpture, a peephole museum, and chewing-gum sculpture. It also contains recipes for baker's dough, fingerpaints, modeling compound, and paste.

MUSIC Even if your child is not involved in a serious program with a musical instrument, you can introduce him to the art of music by listening to records or tapes of folk, country, classical, jazz, and rock music. *Making Musical Instruments*, by Rebecca Anders, with pictures by G. Overlie (Lerner, 1975), shows ways of making simple percussion, wind, and stringed instruments from household items. *Jug Bands and Homemade Music*, by James Collier (Grosset and Dunlap, 1973), explains the different elements of music and provides instructions for creating homemade instruments for children in the fifth and sixth grades.

"CHARADES" This is a perennially popular parlor game in which each word or phrase is silently acted out, or pantomimed, by one or more persons while the other players try to guess the word or phrase. The players can pick topics to be acted out, such as names of songs or movie titles. The movie *Gone With the Wind* is a good example. For the word *gone*, the person pretends to leave the room or waves good-bye. For the word *with*, the person picks up something and pretends to take it with him. For the word *wind*, the person fans a magazine to create a breeze. To pantomime a long word, you can also break it down into individual syllables, for example, *musical = mew-sick-al*. Other topics for this game could be: book titles, names of famous people, lines of poetry, advertising slogans, and proverbs.

PUPPET AND MARIONETTE SHOWS You can make simple hand puppets with small paper bags by drawing faces on them. A cardboard packing carton turned on its side, with a curtain over the front and holes cut out of the back for hands, can be a puppet stage. Each family member can make his own puppet and then act out a story by engaging in conversation with the other puppets. *Making Puppets Come Alive*, by Larry Engler and Carol Fijan, with photos by David Attie and designs by Paul Davis (Taplinger, 1974), provides basic puppetry techniques and explains ways to construct simple puppets and stages. *Sticks and Stones and Ice Cream Cones*, by Phyllis Fiarotta (Workman, 1973), gives plans for creating a complete puppet show.

FAMILY LETTERS   Family letters to relatives or faraway friends can be exciting. The entire family sits at the table, with one person acting as recorder. Each family member contributes information for the letter as well as questions to the person receiving the letter.

EXAMPLE: Dear Aunt Marion and Uncle Joe,
We are writing this letter to you as a family. Jack, who is now ten years old, would like to thank you for the birthday present. Cathy says that she wants you to come visit us for the weekend. [And so on. Let the younger children draw a picture of the family to enclose with the letter.]

FAMILY ALBUM   Paste into a scrapbook photos and souvenirs from family trips, activities, and outings. Have your child write captions for them including the names of the individuals in the photo, the place, and the date. These objects will add a lot to the family's enjoyment in later years.

ORDERING BY MAIL   Together, go through catalogues from Sears and Roebuck, Montgomery Ward, and other stores. Clip coupons from magazines and send away for free booklets on subjects of interest.

PANEL DISCUSSIONS   The entire family can participate in panel discussions. One family member who serves as the panel leader chooses a topic to be discussed and gives the other family members a few days to think about the topic and perhaps dig up some information. The panel leader introduces the topic and asks the other family members questions, leading the discussion. Current news events are good topics to be used.

USING A TAPE RECORDER   If you have a tape recorder, it is fun to tape and then replay family panel discussions, stories, poetry readings, and favorite songs. This activity is good for improving listening skills as well as developing good speech, conversational abilities, and vocabulary.

WRITING SCARY STORIES Each family member contributes a sentence to a short story. To trigger everyone's imagination, provide a thrilling opening sentence such as: "It was getting very dark and cold; the wild animals were growling with hunger; and the children still could not find their way out of the forest."

Family Outings

On weekends and holidays, the family hour can be extended to become the family outing; the entire family can visit a place of mutual interest.

Advance visits to the library can provide relevant information to children that will prepare them to get more out of the experience. During and after the experience children should have ample opportunity for discussion.

Places of interest to most children include the local zoo, the aquarium, the firehouse, the airport, the waterfront (boatyards and docks), museums, amusement parks, botanical gardens, and factories. Also of interest to most children are parks, bridges, antique shops, flea markets, craft and hobby stores, bakeries, garden stores and greenhouses, fairgrounds, public buildings, police stations, post offices, newspapers, radio and television stations, and almost anyplace where grown-ups—particularly parents—work. You might like to visit a farm—explore the meadows, fields, and woods and observe the animals or visit a dairy.

You might like to try camping. *The Boy Scout Handbook* is, of course, a reliable and comprehensive guide. And you don't even have to take a real trip. There's a lot you can practice, sleeping out in your own backyard.

You can also take a "trip" at home by bird-watching. Hang bird feeders from a safe place, such as a tree. Fill them with sunflower seeds or mixed bird seed; provide water and suet. Many different kinds of birds will probably come to your feeders. A paperback bird guide will give you enough information to identify most of them, and a pair of inexpensive binoculars will allow parent and child to observe details of appearance, behavior, and habitat.

Bicycle trips are fun, and many localities now have bicycle lanes and special maps showing interesting and safe trips.

For cyclists and noncyclists, historic routes are usually enjoyable and interesting. And after you've seen a bit of local history, you have a good excuse to read more about it and to talk about it at dinner. Ask your local historical society what historic spots there are around you; or try the local chamber of commerce—they may have some ideas, too.

What about a family outing to engage in some sport or athletic activity such as swimming, boating, ice skating, tennis, skiing, or roller-skating? Or you can have an "outing" at home—play horseshoes, beanbag, croquet, badminton, or ball games in your backyard or in a nearby park. And how about a treasure hunt? Hide clues around the neighborhood, yard, house, or apartment that lead to a "treasure" hidden nearby.

If you want to go much farther afield than your backyard, neighborhood or locality, you might like to consult the Mobil Travel Guides, which describe places of interest all over the United States. Or you can get booklets from a local travel agent describing trips parents and children might enjoy together. (Chapter 6 contains suggestions about appropriate trips for children at different grade levels.)

Traveling in the Car

Long car trips can often be tedious to children and therefore aggravating to parents. The familiar words "Mommy, when are we going to get there" have been heard by almost every parent. One way to deal with this dilemma is to have your child bring along a "learning travel kit." Using an old suitcase or strong shopping bag, have him fill it with a few story books from the library, paper and pencil, crayons and scissors, and any games that can be played in the car.

Besides these activities for the child there are many car games that can be played:

"ALPHABET SEARCH"   The object of this game is to identify something along the road that begins with each letter of the alphabet. Each person begins by looking for an object that begins with the letter A, such as an automobile. The first person to identify an object that begins with A then goes on to the letter B. The other players must discover a different object that begins with A before they can go on to B. The first player to reach Z is the winner.

"NAVIGATOR" As you drive, let your child act as your navigator. With a notebook and pencil your child can record mileage readings, miles covered each hour, the amount of gasoline and oil needed, the cost in tolls, amount of time spent in road stops. Show him how to read a map, and he can trace your journey with a magic marker. Have him estimate the distance using the mileage table on the map and guess when you will come upon the map locations. Have him list all cities and towns, route numbers and places of interest that are on the map and check them off as you come upon the signs for them along the road. Your child can include all of this information, as well as pictures taken, postcards acquired, and his own thoughts and feelings about the trip in his "Vacation Diary" or "Navigator's Log."

"LICENSE PLATES" Look for license plates from different states, plates that contain digits that when added together give the number 10 or some other number, plates of different colors. Read mottoes on different plates. Look for cars of different colors and makes as well.

GAMES Children learn naturally through games. Their verbal and cognitive skills are developed, as is their social awareness, which improves from their abiding by the rules and regulations.

Parents can purchase many different puzzles and board games for a child's birthday and other festive occasions. Manipulative toys are good for younger children, for they not only provide for the child's cognitive development but also give the child practice in hand-eye coordination. Some guidelines that parents can follow in choosing toys for young children are

> In using the toy, is the child an active participant or just a passive observer?
>
> Does the toy enable the child to use his creativity and imagination in one way or another?
>
> Is the toy too simplistic or too complicated for the child at this time in his development?
>
> Will the toy have lasting interest for the child, or will he become tired of it after a short period of time?

Games such as Monopoly, chess, checkers, Parcheesi, and Scrabble can provide many hours of enjoyable learning experiences for older children. Some libraries contain games that can be borrowed as well as books giving the rules for hundreds of interesting and unusual games—indoor and outdoor, verbal and board, quiet and active. Here are some representative titles:

Games for One, Two or More, edited by Margaret and Cameron Yerian (Children's Press, 1974), presents ideas for indoor and outdoor games that require no special equipment. Another book by the same authors, called *Group Games* (Children's Press, 1974), explains the rules of popular and unfamiliar games that can be played by groups, indoors or outdoors.

The Make-It, Play-It Game Book, by Roz Abisch and Boche Kaplan (Walker, 1975), contains directions for making and playing twenty-three easy games by using household odds and ends.

Book of 1,000 Family Games, by the editors of *Reader's Digest* (1971, Reader's Digest Press), is a comprehensive book containing action, board, and verbal games. There are special chapters on teaching and learning, creative games, and games you can make yourself with ordinary materials. It also includes information about magic tricks, quizzes, and brainteasers. Especially valuable are its indexes of games suitable for the physically handicapped and mentally retarded.

Creative Teaching Games, by Linda Polon and Wendy Pollitt (Dennison, 1974), is full of ideas for making games that emphasize basic reading/language skills as well as math games. It gives the reader tips on using materials found in the home.

Scarne's Encyclopedia of Games, by John Scarne (Harper and Row, 1973), is written by the world-famous game authority. It contains over one thousand games played with dice, cards, tiles, and dominoes, as well as lottery and board games.

The World Book of Children's Games, by Arnold Arnold (Fawcett Crest, 1972), is a collection of informal games played by children throughout the world. For children ages four to twelve.

The End?
No!
Only the Beginning!

One of the ulterior motives in presenting these activities for parents to use with their children is to instill in them a spark that will light their imagination. As was previously stated, the activities are meant only as an introduction to the limitless arena of parent-child learning experiences. Each and every parent should use these activities as a stepping stone to their own creations as they formulate a relationship with their child that will enable him to be successful in school.

5

Mathematics

The Old and the New

Traditionally the study of elementary school math was based on rote learning and telling, a process that enabled most students to pass the test but very few to understand the various concepts and relationships of the different aspects of mathematics.

A major change took place in the 1960s with the introduction of what was universally known as "the new math." These changes took place because (a) mathematicians began to realize that although new mathematical concepts were constantly being formulated, none of these advances were finding their way into the schools; and (b) the concern that we were falling behind the Soviet Union in its scientific and technological training following the launching of Sputnik in 1957.

The new math stressed underlying principles rather than procedures; so, children were supposed to understand *how* numbers work. A key feature of this new math was the idea of *sets*, that is, a clearly defined collection of objects or ideas.

By the early 1970s, however, it became more and more evident that this approach was not the answer either. Both children and teachers had a difficult time understanding the rules and abstractions of this new math.

The present-day approach, which often combines the old math with the new, is based on the belief that children learn best by doing, that is, through a process of experimenting, exploring, observing, and discovering for themselves. Through his firsthand experiences with physical objects the child is able to arrive at solutions to problems and thereby attain a better understanding of relationships. In working with children, keep in mind the Chinese proverb "I hear and I forget, I see and I remember, I *do* and I *understand*." From this foundation the young elementary school child can advance his understanding of math into the verbal and symbolic realms.

An important addition to the elementary school math curriculum is the introduction of the *metric system*. Since 1971, when the National Education Association issued the U.S. Metric Study Interim Report, measurement through the use of the metric system as well as measurement in the English system has been stressed in American schools. The starting point of the metric system is the *meter* (abbreviated *m*), which is 39.37 inches, a little longer than a yard. The metric system is easier to work with than the English system of measurement because ten of every unit equals one of the next larger unit. Because the United States is slowly "going metric," parents will find that their children are being given more and more work having to do with the metric system of measurement. See pages 110-117 at the end of the mathematics section for an orientation to this system of measurement.

Prekindergarten and Kindergarten

Much of the math learning that takes place in these grades is of a highly informal nature. The teacher directs the children in noticing the numbers of the everyday world, such as license plates, numbers on classroom doors, addresses in the neighborhood, and the number of children who are present and absent. The children observe these numbers and repeat them after the teacher. Even from stories such as "The Three Little Pigs" and "Snow White and the Seven Dwarfs" the children develop their awareness of the various elementary number names.

Matching games in which children relate one set of objects to a set of related objects, such as chairs and children, hats and coats, forks and plates, enable them to understand the concepts of one-to-one correspondence. From this beginning the children learn the concept of sets or collections of things that go together and the meaning of the word *pair*. They also learn to count collections of objects from one to ten and sometimes up to twenty or thirty.

By using classroom materials such as blocks and beads, the children learn how to name the number of objects in a line without having to count them. From these activities they begin to learn the concepts of size, quantity, and position. The characteristics of a rectangle, triangle, square, and circle are explored, and nonnumerical concepts of half and whole are introduced.

Parents can use the following activities with their children to reinforce what the children learn in school.

COUNTING EVERYTHING   When you're walking down the stairs, count the steps. When you are driving in the car, count the trucks you see. Counting fingers and body parts is a pretty standard procedure, but how about counting raisins in the box, cookies in the package, boxes in the pantry, or peas in the pod? The child's whole environment provides counting experiences when you simply ask the question "How many?"

STRINGING BEADS   Have your child make a string of beads alternating the colors. Let him begin by using only one bead of each color and then instruct him to use two, three, four, or five beads of the same color before alternating to a different color.

Another variation of this activity is for the child to increase the number of beads by one every time he uses a different color. The strung beads would consist of one red, then two green, then three blue, and so on.

Parents can offer round macaroni in place of beads. Have your child color them with paint. Buttons of the same color can also be used.

"JAR JUMBLE"   Save different sized jars and their lids for your child to work with. Such a collection will provide your child the opportunity to practice

> matching the covers to the jars
>
> putting the jars in order from tallest to shortest or from fattest to thinnest
>
> using the lids to trace different sized circles with pencil and paper
>
> filling the jars with specified numbers of counting objects such as marbles, coins, paper clips, and so on.

"ONE THROUGH TEN" Divide a sheet of paper into ten squares. At the bottom of each square write the numbers 1 through 10. Draw any number of objects, from one to ten, in each square, as well as a line on which the child can practice writing the number. Have your child count the number of objects in each square, circle the number, and then practice writing the number on the line.

EXAMPLE:

☆ ☆ ☆	□ □ □ □ □ □ □ □
3 3 3 3 3 3 3	8 8 8 8 8 8 8
1 2 ③ 4 5 6 7 8 9 10	1 2 3 4 5 6 7 ⑧ 9 10

CARDS The familiar game of "War" is an excellent one for young children. All the cards are dealt among the players. (Remove the picture cards to simplify the game.) Each player puts out his top card, and the one with the highest numbered card wins all the cards uncovered. The game goes on until one player wins all the other player's cards.

Other simple card games in which pairs or sets are isolated, such as "Go Fish," are also enjoyable and educational.

NUMBER BOOK Construct a book with your child using the numbers 1 to 10. At the top of each page draw a numeral, for example, 2, and beside it write the word, in this case *two*. Have your child cut pictures from magazines that indicate the appropriate number and paste them on each page. Have your child say the number and then count the items in each picture.

NUMBER POSTERS On a large sheet of cardboard write the numbers 1 to 10 down the left-hand side. Collect items that can be placed next to the numbers, such as pebbles, shells, sticks, buttons, marbles, beans, and macaroni. Keep these items in a cigar box or bag (small Baggies are fine) so that they will not get lost. The child places the proper number of items next to the corresponding number.

CIRCLING NUMBERS   Give your child a red crayon and a magazine and ask him to circle all the 1's, 2's, or 3's he can find. Keep the magazine and have him circle the other numbers with different colors from time to time.

NUMBERS IN THE NEIGHBORHOOD   On your walks throughout the neighborhood point out the numbers on houses and stores, license plates, street signs, and price tags in the stores you visit.

THE IDEA OF THE PAIR   In a large bag or box collect a pair of shoes, socks, mittens, gloves, boots, and so on. Have your child pick the objects from the box and place them in pairs.

A variation on this same theme is to draw pictures of pairs of things, but separating the pair, then have the child draw lines matching the two items of the pair.

MATCHING SHAPES   On a sheet of paper or cardboard trace a square, triangle, circle, and rectangle in different positions. Cut out the same sized shapes from another piece of paper and have the child match the cut-out shapes with those drawn on the paper.

SHAPES OF THE WORLD   Draw and color with your child the things that have the shape of a triangle, circle, square, and rectangle.

EXAMPLES:

Triangle—shape of a Christmas tree, an Indian tepee, the sail of a boat, the cone of an ice-cream cone

Circle—clock, plate, ball, button, balloon, snow man, wheel, the sun, the moon

Square--checkerboard, box, table, floor or ceiling tile

Rectangle—window, book, bed, picture, table top, room, side of house

"GIANT STEPS"   Have your child stand about twenty paces from you. The parent says to the child, "You may take two giant steps." The child says, "May I," and the parent responds either "Yes, you may" or "No, you may not" and then proceeds to give the child another direction such as, "You may take ten little steps." The child takes the steps and counts as he does so. Vary the numbers from one to ten. Children will often pick up this game and play it by themselves.

BIG AND LITTLE, TALL AND SHORT, HIGH AND LOW   To give your child practice in concepts of size and position, have him do the following exercise with you:

On your walks in the neighborhood point out the objects that are big (houses, cars) and little (babies, birds, ants); tall (apartment buildings, telephone poles) and short (fire hydrants, blades of grass); high (clouds, flying airplanes) and low (puddles, fallen leaves).

MANY AND FEW, MORE AND LESS, SAME, NONE   Using cookies, pebbles, buttons, or beads, do some of the following exercises with your child:

1. Pick a number of objects from the pile, place them in a row in front of you, and have your child place the *same* number of objects in front of him. Also do this exercise with *more* and *less*.

2. Have him make piles that have *many* and *few* objects in them.

3. Hide an object in one hand and hide *none* in the other hand. Have your child guess which hand has the object and which hand has *none*.

POSITIONAL CONCEPTS
"On Top Of and Under"
Give your child a book or magazine and have him place it *on top of* the table and then *under* the table. Ask him to hide a button *under* something in the house (a rug, a newspaper). Talk about the things in the house that are *on top of* or *under* other household items, such as the floor under the rug, the bed under the sheets, the radio on top of the table, the roof on top of the house. Using a magazine picture of a room, have your child point out all the things that are on top of or under something else. Using the kitchen sink, a basin, or the bathtub and objects such as a cork, pennies, pieces of wood, a ball, a nail, paper clips, and so on, have your child put into one pile the things that float *on top of* the water and into another pile the things that sink *under* the surface of the water.

"Above and Below"

Play the "What Am I Thinking Of?" game with your child. The parent says: "I am thinking of something that is very small. It comes *above* the ground for food but lives in a home *below* the ground." (An ant.) Or "Its roots are *below* the ground, but its branches are *above* the ground." (A tree.)

"In Front of and Behind"

Put an object down on the table or the floor and have your child place other objects *in front of* and *behind* it. Look at pictures and point out the things that are *in front of* and *behind* other things in the picture.

"Middle"

Draw pictures of three cars, five ducks, the fingers on one hand, a sandwich, seven houses, and so on, and have your child color or circle those things that are in the *middle*.

"CAN YOU MATCH ME?"   Using counters that can be assembled and dismantled easily, such as straws, pencils, buttons, beads, toothpicks, or strips of paper, make a design and have your child construct the same design alongside yours. Start with simple crosses or squares; as your child becomes proficient, you can make more elaborate designs.

"AM I WHOLE?"   Paste pictures of people, things, and animals on three-by-five index cards. Cut the cards in half, shuffle them and place them facedown. The first player chooses two cards. If they match to make a whole, he keeps them and goes again. When they do not match to make a whole, the cards are placed in the deck, and the next player tries.

COUNTING SONGS   Starting with closed fists, lift the appropriate finger as you sing this song with your child:

> "One little, two little, three little Indians,
> Four little, five little, six little Indians,
> Seven little, eight little, nine little Indians,
> Ten little Indian boys and girls."

Once again lift the appropriate finger while you sing

"One, one, here is my thumb,
Two, two, look at my shoe,
Three, three, point to me,
Four, four, where is the floor,
Five, five, I am five,
Six, six, pick up sticks,
Seven, seven, up in heaven,
Eight, eight, close the gate,
Nine, nine, I feel fine,
Ten, ten, let's clap to ten."

PICTURE AND STORY BOOKS   When reading stories to your child, you can easily reinforce the elementary number concepts by pointing out the various objects and characters and having him count them. Point out the various shapes also. Here is a list of good books for this.

The Berenstain Bear's Counting Book, by Stanley and Janice Berenstain (Random House, 1976), illustrates the numbers from 1 to 10 with the antics of a hockey team.

One, Two, Three, by Marc Brown (Little, Brown, 1976), pictures animals in groups for teaching children about the numbers 1 to 20.

Teddy Bears 1 to 10, by Susanna Grotz (Follett, 1969), is an amusing book of the numbers up to 10.

Monster Bubbles, A Counting Book, by Dennis Nolan (Prentice-Hall, 1976), shows different monsters taking turns blowing bubbles in amounts from 1 to 20.

First Grade

In the first grade, children usually learn the whole numbers through fifty and count up to fifty by ones, by twos, by fives, and by tens. The concept of even and odd numbers is learned. Comparison terms such as *more, fewer, as many as, greater than,* and *less than* are expanded. Simple addition and subtraction of whole numbers are learned; whole objects are divided into halves, thirds, and fourths, and position terms such as *inside, outside, on, vertical,* and *horizontal* are explored.

The relationship of pennies, nickels, dimes, and quarters, telling time by the hour and half hour, the relationship of days to weeks and days to months, and temperature and weight are studied.

Measurement terms of inch, foot, quart, and gallon are worked with. Many school districts introduce the metric units of meter and centimeter during this school year in a highly informal manner through simple activities such as having the children measure each other as well as the size of their hands, feet, waist, and arms.

The geometric shapes that were learned in kindergarten are reviewed, as well as the relationship of sets and subsets. A number line (_____1 2 3 4 5 6 7 8 9 10_____) is used as one of the ways to help children see what is happening when addition and subtraction is taking place, and simple word problems are begun.

ESTIMATING BEANS   Collect an assortment of different containers in various shapes (a glass, a cup, a small box, a funnel, etc.). Fill one container with dried beans (marbles, pebbles, and buttons are fine, too) and have each family member guess the amount. Then have your child count the beans. The person whose estimate is closest to the real amount is the winner. Repeat the same activity with the other containers.

PLACE VALUE OF NUMBERS   Make up two sets of number cards from 0 to 9 or buy a set of flash cards at the variety store. Place them in front of your child and call out any number from ten to ninety-nine. (Example: "seventy-eight.") The child must arrange the cards to show the correct number.

BUNDLING TENS   Get a large collection of popsicle sticks, tongue depressors, or toothpicks. Have your child use rubber bands to bunch tens together. With collections of tens and nine separate individual sticks, you can play simple games that teach numeration. Ask the child to take varying bunches of tens and ones, and to find out how many sticks he has in all. He will need to count them one by one at first. Later he will learn to count by tens. You might want to use a chart to record the results of your child's work.

EXAMPLE:	Number of Bunches of Tens	Number of Individual Ones	Total Number of Sticks
∦∦∦∦ ∦∦∦∦ ∦∦∦∦ ∦∦∦∦		/ / /	
	4	3	43
∦∦∦∦ ∦∦∦∦		/ /	
	2	2	22

ADDITION WITH COUNTERS   Draw three large rectangles on a sheet of paper with a plus sign (+) in between the first two rectangles and an equal sign (=) between the last two rectangles.

EXAMPLE:

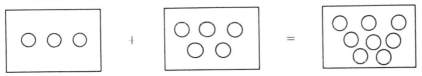

Give your child counters (dried beans, toothpicks, buttons) and ask him to place a specified number of counters in each of the first two rectangles and then count out and place an amount equal to their sum in the third rectangle.

This exercise can be done with subtraction and multiplication problems also.

"TARGET ADDITION"   On a large piece of heavy cardboard construct a game board that looks like this:

	Add 5 points			
Take an extra turn	1	12	3	6
	9	7	5	10
	15	2	4	8
	Lose 3 points			Lose a turn

Each player takes a turn pitching a penny at the board from three feet away. The numeral that the marker lands on is added to his score. The first player to reach 100 is the winner.

"BINGO"   The entire family can play Bingo. Divide a sheet of paper or cardboard into ten squares and write in each square any number between one and fifty. Make five of these Bingo cards, making sure you have used all of the numbers from one to fifty. On small pieces of paper that are sized to just cover the numbered squares, again write the numbers from one to fifty. These will be the markers. Place the numbered markers in a box and have each family member take a turn picking a marker and calling out the number. The person who has a Bingo card with the number just called on it is given the marker to cover that number on his card. The first person to cover all the numbers on his card is the winner.

MARBLE COUNTING   On the floor, place a string two feet long in the shape of a circle. Give your child ten marbles to roll into the circle from a short distance away. After the child rolls his marbles, he must count the number in the circle and the number outside of the circle. Then the parent plays. Have the child mark down the results on a sheet of paper.

A variation that gives additional counting practice can be introduced by assigning different values to different colored marbles—for example, red marbles are worth two points, blues get five points, and greens get ten points. The child must figure out the number of points each player has earned.

EVEN AND ODD   Review with your child the concept of odd and even. Even numbers are 2, 4, 6, 8, and so on, because each of these numbers can be divided into two groups, each having an equal number in it. For example, 4 can be divided into two equal groups of 2 and 2; 6 can be divided into two equal groups of 3 and 3. Demonstrate this to your child by using marbles, pieces of paper, or other countable items. The odd numbers 1, 3, 5, 7, 9, and so on, do not have this property. Ask your child such questions as

"Is there an odd or even number of chairs in the room?"

"Are the number of fingers on one hand odd or even? How about two hands?"

Here are two games that reinforce the idea of odd and even.

1. Using a set of dice, have your child pick either the odd numbers or the even numbers. Whatever your child picks, you take the opposite. The two players take turns throwing the dice. When the two dice both show odd numbers, the individual who chose odd is the winner and gets one point. The same applies when the dice show even numbers. The first player to get fifteen points is the winner.

2. This game can be played with toothpicks, bottle caps, dried beans, pebbles, or any other small objects. Each player starts the game with twenty-five objects. The first player places a few objects in

his hand without showing the other player. The second player must guess if the number of hidden objects is odd or even. If his guess is correct, he wins the objects. If he is wrong, then he must give that number of objects to his opponent. The second player then hides a quantity of objects in his hand, and the first player must guess odd or even. The first to collect all of his opponent's objects is the winner.

COUNTING BY TWOS, FIVES, AND TENS

1. Divide a sheet of paper into twenty-five squares. Write the numbers from 2 to 50, counting by twos and leaving a blank for every third or fourth number. The child must fill in the blanks.

EXAMPLE: 2, 4, ___, 8, 10, ___, 14, . . .
Do this counting by fives and tens also.

EXAMPLE: 5, 10, ___, 20, 25, ___, 35, ___, 45, 50.
10, 20, ___, 40, ___.

2. Lightly trace a picture in pencil and place dots every inch along the line. Then erase the pencil line and label each dot with numbers, counting either by twos, fives, or tens. The child must connect the dots from number to number to find out what the picture is.

EXAMPLE:

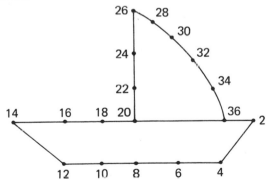

Inexpensive "follow-the-dots" books can be acquired at your local variety store.

"WHAT NUMBER AM I THINKING OF?" Using the numbers between one and fifty, ask your child questions such as

"I am thinking of the number that comes before nineteen. What number am I thinking of?"

"The number that comes after thirty-nine."

"The number that is three less than five."

"The number that is five more than ten."

"FIND THE NUMBERS" Make up number cards from 1 to 50 by writing each number on a three-by-five index card. Write the number word on the back of each card. (Parents may wish to purchase these cards. They are usually available in stationery and toy stores.) Shuffle the cards and have your child place them in order.

Ask your child to give you the even cards; the odd cards.

Ask him for the cards from nineteen to thirty-nine.

Ask him for the number words *seven*, *eleven*, and *fifty*.

Ask him for any numbers that contain a five, such as five, fifteen, twenty-five, thirty-five, forty-five, and fifty.

Ask him to show you three numbers that when added together will make the number fifteen.

PICTURE GAMES Draw pictures of five cups and six saucers, eight bats and seven balls, six feet and eight shoes, and so on, asking the child, "How many more are needed?" Have your child draw in the missing objects, that is, one cup, one ball, two feet, to complete the pairs.

"MAKE YOUR OWN CALENDAR" Give your child crayons, and a large sheet of paper. Fold the paper in half. The top half is for a picture. Encourage your child to draw a picture to correspond with each month of the year, for example, a picture of snowmen and sleigh riding for January. Make enough squares for the correct number of days as well as squares for the names of the days of the week. Have your child fill in the calendar using a regular calendar as a guide. This is a good project at the start of each month, and can be enlivened by putting in national and local holidays, birthdays of family and friends, and forthcoming events important to the child.

MONEY BOOK Cut out pictures of items that would cost from one to ten cents, or have your child draw different pictures of such things as gum candy, marbles, potato chips, and so on. Write an estimated price under each item. The child must tell you the proper number of coins needed to make up the cost of the items. Use play money or real coins.

BODY MEASUREMENT   Experience with nonstandard units of measure is important to the development of measurement concepts. Have your child use various parts of his body to measure the world around him. "How many of *his* feet long is the living room? How many arm spans long is the couch?" The distance from elbow to middle fingertip or from shoulder to elbow are possible units of measure. The child discovers that nonstandard units of measure make comparison difficult because of different arm, hand and feet size.

Measurements and How We Use Them, by Tillie Pine and Joseph Levine, with pictures by Harriet Sherman (McGraw-Hill, 1974), teaches young children about the importance of taking accurate measurements and about the tools used in measuring.

"CONCENTRATION"   To give your child practice in recognizing numbers and to improve his memory skills, play the traditional game of concentration with him. Using a standard deck of playing cards, lay all the cards facedown on the table. Arrange them in several rows. The first player turns any two cards faceup. If the two cards are a pair, he keeps them. If they don't match, he turns them facedown again on the table in their original positions. Then the second player takes a turn, and the play continues until all the cards have been taken.

Second Grade

In the second grade, children usually begin counting by hundreds. They add numbers up to ninety-nine and learn how addition and subtraction are related to each other. Number lines are used to demonstrate the relationship between addition and subtraction. The children also study the relationship of different temperatures in terms of degrees. They learn multiplication as they count by twos, by threes, by fours, and by fives. They continue their understanding of fractional parts of a whole by experimentation with halves, thirds, and quarters of a whole.

They learn the relationships between: meter and centimeter; half inch, inch, and foot; pennies, nickels, dimes, quarters, half-dollars, and dollars; dozen and half dozen; ounces and pounds. They review the concepts of hour and half hour, learn the relationship of minutes to hours, and learn the concepts of "quarter after" and "quarter to" and "minutes after" and "minutes to" the hour.

"DON'T CROSS ME"   On a large sheet of paper write the numbers 1 to 30 two times, scattering them all over the page. The first player draws a line connecting the two number 1's. Then the second player draws a line connecting the two number 2's, and so on. The rule of the game is that in connecting the number pairs a player cannot cross a line that is already drawn. The first player who cannot connect a pair of numbers without crossing a line is the loser.

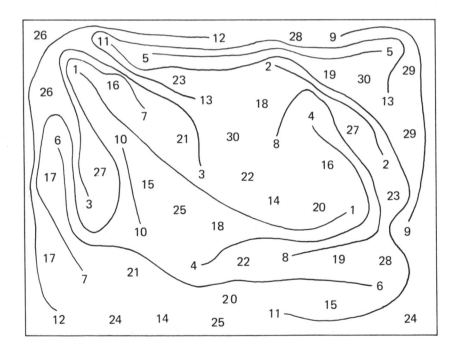

"HOW MUCH IS IT?"   Using real money or play money from the dime store, go over with your child the value of each coin or bill. Make up item cards with pictures of items from a magazine and the "price" of the article. Give your child the money box and lay the card down with the picture side up. Your child has to place the correct amount of money on the picture.

MULTIPLICATION DICE To give your child practice in multiplication from 1 to 6, have him make up two playing mats that look like the following:

X	1	2	3	4	5	6
1						
2						
3						
4						
5						
6						

Each player takes a turn rolling a pair of dice and then multiplying the two numbers shown on the dice. The answer is placed on the grid in the appropriate row and column that correspond to the numbers on the dice. The winner is the first player to complete the grid. (Older children could use such a grid to tally probability of various combinations after several hundred rolls of the dice.)

MATCHING NUMBERS To give your child practice in recognizing numbers as well as in being precise when he is working with them, write down two columns of numbers. Make some of the numbers in each column exactly alike and some slightly different. Have your child circle the numbers that are exactly alike.

EXAMPLE:

483	438
(20,168	20,168)
5,932	5,923
(845	845)
(67,842,305	67,842,305)

"TOSS IT, COUNT IT"   Turn a chair upside down and attach a piece of paper, each with a different number, onto each leg. Have your child make rings by cutting out and discarding the middles of plastic coffee-container tops or heavy cardboard. Each player stands about six feet from the chair and takes four turns attempting to toss the rings onto the chair legs. After his four tries he adds up the numbers to find out his score. The player with the highest score after a number of turns is the winner.

This game can be played for practice in multiplication by having the players score the product of the numbers they ring. If three legs are rung, the score would be the product of those three numbers.

"PICK-UP STICKS"   Using the commercial game of "Pick-Up Sticks" (available in toy stores), assign a different value to each stick color. (For example, red sticks count as 3, blue sticks count as 5, and so on.) Each player takes a turn picking up the sticks with the white stick provided. After his turn is over, he either adds or multiplies— according to some preestablished rule—the values of his acquired sticks to find his total. The player with the highest score is the winner.

Any number values can be assigned to the different colors in order to make the game conform to any grade level.

"MATCH IT"   On three-by-five index cards write different math problems, and on other cards write the answers.

EXAMPLE:

Make up thirty sets of cards. Select the math problems from your child's textbook. Each player takes a turn picking one card from each deck. If the problem and the answer go together, he keeps the cards. If they do not, he returns the cards to their respective decks, and the next player goes. The player with the most cards at the end of the game is the winner. Such cards can be made up with any and all types of math problems and for any grade level.

"THE FASTEST WAY"   Using toothpicks, straws, or any countable objects the parent and child can practice making sets to help the child understand that multiplication is simply a faster way to add than counting all the objects.

Have the child make four groupings of two items each. On counting the objects, the child will see that there are eight items. Explain to him that since each set has two items and there are four sets, we can find the answer faster by simply multiplying the four sets by the two items in each set.

Don't be concerned if it takes your child a while to grasp the idea; through manipulation of the items in this way he will eventually understand.

SHAPES   Make a question-and-answer booklet with your child. Take blank pieces of drawing paper and write down simple questions or instructions at the bottom of the page. The child uses a pencil, ruler, and crayons to complete each page.

EXAMPLES:

1. Draw, color, and name a shape that has four equal sides.

2. Draw a page of all the circular objects that you can think of.

3. Make a triangular robot that can walk, talk, and fly.

4. Draw a picture of a freight train. What shapes are the freight cars?

"ONE MINUTE AT A TIME"   Have your child construct his own clock with paper, crayons, scissors, cardboard, and paper fasteners (for attaching the clock hands). Tell him to use one of the clocks in the house as a model. Move the minute hands with him from notch to notch so he becomes aware that there are sixty minutes in each hour, and let him position the clock to coincide with the real time throughout the day—dinnertime, playtime, bedtime. Whenever you are noticing the time, say to him, "Look, it is five minutes after seven. The big hand is on the one, and the little hand is pointing to the seven."

Draw ten small clocks on a page without the hands. Under each clock write the time you wish the clock to show, and have your child draw the missing hands.

"THE ARROW GAME"   Construct a number line from 0 to 9. Draw two arrows, the first to a number and the second arrow starting from where the first arrow stopped. Point out that the number on which the second arrow stops is the answer to the addition.

EXAMPLE:

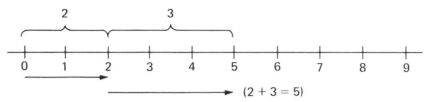

$(2 + 3 = 5)$

Have your child draw arrows to show different sums. Beginning from the other end of the line the child can draw arrows to show problems in subtraction.

COOKING   Cooking experiences can be valuable for all children. Doubling, tripling, or halving recipes are real-life uses of arithmetic. If you are quartering apples, how many quarters will you get from three apples? If a recipe makes two dozen cookies and you need ½ teaspoon of sugar for each cookie, how much sugar will you need to make three dozen? When the right questions are asked of children, an ordinary routine can become an exciting learning experience. (See Chapter 7 for additional ideas in cooking.)

Third Grade

In the third grade, children learn to count by thousands and add and subtract three-digit numbers. They learn the fractional concepts of sixths and eighths of a whole and the properties of plane figures such as the quadrilateral, rectangle, square, and triangle.

Relationships between inches, feet, and yards; pints, quarts, and gallons; and the fractional parts of a pound are explored. Advancing their knowledge of telling time, they learn the five-minute intervals and the meaning of A.M. and P.M.

Rounding off numbers to the nearest hundred is learned. Word problems become more complex, dealing with multiplication and division. Multiplication facts (tables) are learned, and the basic facts of division, using the divisors 1 to 9, are studied. The role in multiplication and division of 0 and 1 are also examined.

"THREE THOUSAND TO WIN"   Parent and child each have a score sheet. The child rolls three dice, one at a time, and writes down the three numbers, in the order of the throw, as a three-place number. Then the parent rolls the three dice. The next three numbers rolled by each player are added to the first score. The first person to reach three thousand is the winner.

PUTTING NUMBERS IN ORDER   Write down fifty numbers between 1,000 and 10,000 in random order. The child must rearrange the numbers in order from the lowest to the greatest number. Reverse the process by asking the child to write a new set of numbers from the greatest to the smallest.

MAKING CHANGE   Give your child some pennies, nickels, dimes, and quarters and have him find different ways to make a certain sum.

EXAMPLE: "Find six different ways to make sixteen cents."
Answer: one dime, one nickel, one penny
two nickels, six pennies
three nickels, one penny
sixteen pennies
one nickel, eleven pennies
one dime, six pennies

LOCATE THE NUMBERS IN THE SHAPE   Draw a circle, square, rectangle, and triangle so that each shape is partly overlapping the others. Write the numbers 1 to 50 in the shapes. Have your child answer questions such as:

Which numbers are in the square?
List the even numbers found in the circle;
Find the sum of the numbers in the rectangle, triangle and square.

"ANIMAL RACE"   To give your child practice in using the number line, play "Animal Race" with him. Draw a number line from 1 to 100. Write the numbers from 1 to 10 on separate pieces of paper with the symbols + or − before the number and a short comment concerning the symbol.

EXAMPLE: +3   running well
+5   picking up speed
+10 take a short cut
−5   tripped on a log
−8   caught in a hunter's trap
−3   stop for a drink of water

Each player chooses an animal and then takes turns picking a piece of paper, without looking, and moving his cardboard or plastic animal along the number line according to the instructions. The first animal to reach 100 is the winner of the race.

EXAMPLE:

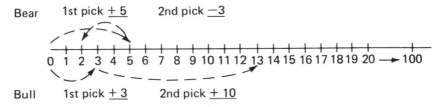

Bear   1st pick + 5   2nd pick −3

0 1 2 3 4 5 6 7 8 9 10 11 12 13 14 15 16 17 18 19 20 → 100

Bull   1st pick + 3   2nd pick + 10

PLACE VALUE   Give your child different sets of numbers and have him arrange them in the highest quantity possible as well as the lowest quantity possible.

EXAMPLES: 5   7   3   1
7   5   3   1 (highest quantity possible)
1   3   5   7 (lowest quantity possible)
2   6   3   9   1   7   9
9   9   7   6   3   2   1 (highest quantity possible)
1   2   3   6   7   9   9 (lowest quantity possible)

READING AND WRITING NUMBERS   For practice in reading and writing numbers give your child some of the following exercises:

1. Write the following numbers:
five hundred sixty-two ____
seventy five thousand sixty-nine ____

2. Write the words for these numbers:

509 _____

2,500 _____

62,890 _____

When your child is learning the higher numbers in later grades, you can use this same exercise for hundreds (make up three sets of number cards from 0 to 9), thousands (four sets), ten thousands (five sets), and hundred thousands (six sets).

EXAMPLE: Called number is "six thousand eight hundred ninety-four." Cards show   [6] [8] [9] [4]

"MY DAILY TIME BOOKLET"   Have your child make a time booklet of his daily schedule by drawing large clocks on separate sheets of paper and labeling them with a sentence telling what he does at that particular time of day.

EXAMPLE:

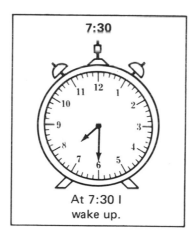

Other pages might state:

At 8:00 I eat breakfast.
At 8:30 I go to school.
At 12:00 I eat lunch.
At 7:30 I watch TV.

PROBLEM SOLVING   Once children can count, they can begin to use their skill to deal with situations that arise in real life. They learn to translate the vocabulary of word problems into actions that solve the problems. If there are cookies to share, turn the experience into a problem for children to solve.

> EXAMPLE: "Suppose I have twenty-five cookies to share among five children. How many will each child get?"
>
> Help your child take twenty-five cookies or counters and divide them into five collections.

Children can learn to reason with the support of counters to solve other types of problems.

> EXAMPLES: "You have five trucks, and I have four trucks. How many do we have all together?"
>
> "If you are making a snowman family that has five members, how many pieces of coal will you need to make their eyes?"
>
> "If I have eight marbles and you have ten, how many more marbles do you have than I have?"
>
> "You want to buy the newspaper, which costs fifteen cents. You only have ten cents. How much more money do you need to buy the paper?"

"FIND THE MISSING NUMBER"   To give your child practice in counting numbers from 1,000 to 10,000, have him fill in the missing numbers on a sheet of paper that you have prepared for him.

> EXAMPLE: 1100, 1200, ___, 1400, 1500, ___, 1700, ___, ___, 2000, 2100, ___, 2300, 2400, ___, ___, 2700, ___, 2900, ___.

"DIVISORS CAN WIN"   Using yellow and blue construction paper, make up a set of division cards. Put the division problem on the blue cards ($3\overline{)6}$) and the answer 2 on the yellow cards. All the blue cards are laid facedown in one area, and all the yellow cards are laid facedown in another area. The object is to pick the blue card, then the yellow, and see if they match. When they match, the player keeps both cards and picks again. When they do not match, the cards are placed facedown in the same spot (another variation on "Concentration"). The player who pairs up the most cards is the winner.

"TELL ME YOUR PROBLEM"   Make up a set of cards with different numbers and instructions on each card. The child has to make up a word problem to go along with the instructions.

> EXAMPLE: One card may say, "Apples, peaches, pears; multiplication problem 2, 3, 6." The child makes up a statement such as "Harry bought two apples at fifteen cents each, three peaches at twenty-five cents each, and six pears at thirty cents. How much did he spend?"

MULTIPLICATION TABLES   Remove the face cards from a pack of playing cards and use the numbered cards from 1 to 10. Each player draws one card to determine who is the dealer. The player with the highest card becomes the dealer. The dealer turns over two cards at a time, and the player who is the first to give the correct product of these two numbers keeps the cards. The winner is the player with the most cards at the end of the game. The winner becomes the dealer.

FRACTIONS WITH PICTURES   Have your child write fractions that explain the pictures you have drawn.

EXAMPLES:

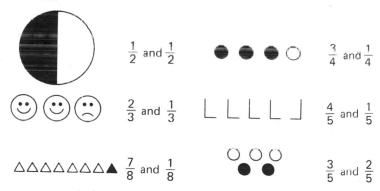

"MONOPOLY"   This game by Parker Brothers is familiar to almost everyone. The use of money to acquire property combined with the development of a strategy to acquire the assets of the other players in the game, along with a good degree of luck in rolling the dice, can provide many hours of enjoyable learning for the entire family. You can purchase a Monopoly game at your local toy store.

Monopoly will give your child practice in:

> counting money as he buys and sells property
> addition and subtraction as he figures out if he has enough money to buy the property he desires

the importance of investing wisely if one is to receive proper dividends (Boardwalk and Park Place are a better bet than Mediterranean and Baltic Avenues.)

making decisions concerning how to invest (houses? hotels?) based on the amount of his available cash and an approximation of his expected income

Fourth Grade

In the fourth grade, children usually learn to work with numbers in the ten thousands and hundred thousands. They expand their knowledge of rounding off numbers to the nearest ten thousand and work with this concept in rounding off money to the nearest dollar. They add and subtract using numbers in the ten thousands. They multiply (both horizontally and vertically) numbers of 1,000 or more by numbers less than 10, as well as using dollars and cents in multiplication problems. In their division exercises they use divisors up to 9 with dividend numbers in the thousands. The divisor 1 and the dividend 0 are also explored.

Fifths, tenths, ninths, and twelfths of a whole are examined, and children learn to use fractions in addition and subtraction problems, as well as multiplying fractions by a whole number.

Work on area is begun. Linear measurement involves fractional parts of an inch, and the concept of the mile is examined. The ton as a unit of weight is learned. Telling time now involves working with seconds in a minute and recording written time. Knowledge of the calendar includes the number of days and weeks in a year. Freezing and boiling points are explored, and the concept of graphs is developed.

"WHICH IS GREATER?"   Have your child make up fifty three-by-five index cards with mathematics problems in addition, subtraction, multiplication, and division. Divide the cards equally among all the players. Each player turns over one card, works the problem mentally, and announces the answer to the others. The player whose problem gives the highest answer wins all the cards. The player with the most cards at the end of the game is the winner.

"WHAT DATE IS IT?"   Make up a series of question cards to be used with a calendar. Place the answer to the question on the opposite side of the card. The child picks a card and uses the calendar to find the answer.

EXAMPLES:

Which date shows the fourth Friday in the month of March?

Which date shows the second Tuesday in the month of February?

Which date shows one week after May 17?

How many Sundays are there in the month of January?

How many Thursdays are there in the month of September?

Which month has only twenty-eight days?

Which months have thirty-one days?

On what day of the week will Christmas fall this year?

On what day of the week will the birthdays of the members of our family fall this year?

How many days are there between July 26 and August 14?

"NUMBERONI"   Using macaroni shells and dried beans, make up a key showing what each shell and bean stands for. The different kinds of beans might represent ones, tens, hundreds, and the macaroni shells could represent thousands, ten thousands, and hundred thousands. The key would look like this:

lima beans	ones
kidney beans	tens
navy beans	hundreds
elbow macaronis	thousands
ziti	ten thousands
shell macaronis	hundred thousands

Using the key, the child must sort the counters into the correct order and state the number in following the parent's instructions. An example could be: "Using counters, show me the following number: 246,531." The child uses one lima bean, three kidney beans, five navy beans, six elbow macaroni, four ziti, and two shell macaroni, in right-to-left order.

"ANSWER MY QUESTIONS"   Give your child a list of ten numbers and make up a list of questions that pertain to the numbers.

EXAMPLE: 145   365

             2579   800

             45,804   796,752

             236   25

             220   459,754,382

Which is the largest number?

Which is the smallest number?

Which two numbers, when added together, will give a third numbers from this list? (145 + 220 = 365)

Which numbers have a two in the ten's place? (220, 25)

Which number relates to the calendar? (365 days in a year)

Which number can be divided by another number to give the answer 32? (800 ÷ 25 = 32)

Which number is a little less than 800,000? How much less?

Which two numbers, when multiplied together, will give the product 36,643,200? (45,804 × 800)

Rearrange the digits in 459,754,382 to form the smallest possible number. (234,455,789)

Find the sum of all the numbers.

SYMBOLS   List a number of math problems containing the numbers and answers but leaving out the symbols of the different mathematical procedures. Have your child experiment with different combinations until he finds the right combination of signs that will give him the correct answer.

EXAMPLES: 3   4   3 =   4   (3+4−3=4)

               22 10 13 = 233   (22×10+13=233)

            100   5   3 =   60   (100÷5×3=60)

              7   7   7 =   7   (7×7÷7=7)

A commercial card game called "Krypto," which can be purchased at local game stores, expands this idea. In "Krypto" five cards with numbers on them are dealt to each player. A goal card is turned over. The idea is for each player to use all of five number cards in an equation whose answer is the goal number. For example, if you are dealt 17, 3, 8, 2, 1, with a goal of 10, one possible equation would be

$$17 - ([8 \div 2] \times 1 + 3) = 10$$

Each dealt hand will have several possible solutions. See how many you and your child can develop.

BAR GRAPHS Have your child look through the newspapers for some examples of bar graphs, cut them out, and paste them on construction paper. Go over the graphs with him so that he understands their meaning.

Use an almanac to find statistics, such as the ten most populated countries in the world, the largest cities in the country, the states with the greatest population, and other facts that can be presented on a graph. Have your child make up graphs with these facts and then give him questions that he must answer by using his graph.

Your child can keep bar graphs on almost any subject. Have him make up his own bar graph book to keep graphs on subjects that interest him. Some topics you might suggest are

> batting averages of his favorite baseball players
>
> the number of books he reads each month
>
> how he spends his allowance
>
> the population of various countries, states, or cities
>
> the distance of the planets from the sun

EQUATIONS Take a large piece of paper and draw any number about three inches high right in the middle of the page. Have your child write down on the same sheet of paper as many equations as he can think of for that number. If you write down the number 100, your child could write equations such as

$$10 \times 10 = 100$$
$$1000 \div 10 = 100$$
$$50 + 25 + 25 = 100$$
$$250 - 150 = 100$$

The number of equations are limitless. See how many your child can do in five minutes. "TUF" (Avalon Hill Co.) is a widely available commercial game that involves making such equations.

THE PYTHAGOREAN SQUARE A Pythagorean square is nothing more than a square array of the numbers from 1 to 100. Children of all ages can use this square to reinforce their school learning, depending on what math level they are on. Have your child make his own square.

1	2	3	4	5	6	7	8	9	10
11	12	13	14	15	16	17	18	19	20
21	22	23	24	25	26	27	28	29	30
31	32	33	34	35	36	37	38	39	40
41	42	43	44	45	46	47	48	49	50
51	52	53	54	55	56	57	58	59	60
61	62	63	64	65	66	67	68	69	70
71	72	73	74	75	76	77	78	79	80
81	82	83	84	85	86	87	88	89	90
91	92	93	94	95	96	97	98	99	100

Investigate the square with your child by asking some of the following questions:

How many numbers are there in each row? in each column?

Which numbers have a 5 (or 3, 8, 9, etc.) in the unit position? (5, 15, 25, 35, 45, 55, 65, 75, 85, 95)

Which numbers have a 5 in both positions? (55)

If the square went from the number 1 to the number 1,000,000, which numbers would then have a 5 in all positions? (55; 555; 5,555; 55,555; 555,555)

Lightly circle the even numbers. What kind of pattern is formed?

Lightly circle the odd numbers. What pattern do we see now?

If you draw a diagonal line between 1 and 100, what can we discover about all the numbers that touch the line?

1   (the unit numbers go from 1 to 9; the tens numbers go
   12   from 1 to 10; each number is 11 more than the
     23   previous number; if you add 1 to the number in
       34   the tens position, you get the number in the
         45   unit position, for example, 23/2+1=3,
           56   89/8+1=9)
             67
               78
                 89
                   100

If you draw a diagonal line between 10 and 91, what can we discover about all the numbers that touch the line?

(the unit numbers decrease from 9 to 1; the tens num-   10
bers increase from 1 to 9; each number is 9 more   19
than the previous number; the two digits of each   28
number, except 10, when added together   37
equal 10, for example, 37/3+7=10, 64/   46
6+4=10; if we multiply the unit   55
number by the tens number, we   64
get an interesting series of   73
products: 82

91

(1, 9, 16, 21, 24, 25, 24, 21, 16, 9)

Have your child draw lines between two other numbers and look for other relationships.

In what column and row is the number 67 located?

Which numbers can be divided by 5 (or any other number) evenly? (5, 10, 15, 20, 25, etc.) What kind of pattern is formed? What pattern do we see for the positions of the multiples of other numbers?

What multiples show a diagonal pattern? (3 and 9)

Circle the prime numbers. (A prime number is a number that can be divided evenly by itself and also by 1. They are 2, 5, 7, 11, 13, 17, 19, 23, 29, 31, 37, 41, 43, 47, 53, 59, 61, 67, 71, 73, 79, 83, 89, 97.)

How many factors can you circle for the number 24? (2, 4, 6, 8, 12, 24) All of these numbers can be divided evenly into the number 24.

Circle number patterns on the square, having your child figure out the pattern and then complete it.

EXAMPLES: 3, 6, 9, 12, . . .   (15, 18, 21, 24, 27, 30, . . .)
                 1, 2, 4, 8, 16, . . .   (32, 64)
                 1, 7, 13, 19, 25, . . .   (31, 37, 43, 49, . . .)

"DIVISION JOURNEY"   Have your child make up a game board like the following:

Start	36	4	45	9	7	57	42	22	15	20

77	32	3	28	81	56	12	96	35	22		48

21										18

Finish

	63	100	14	84	50	47	16	8	

6									24

30	27	48	3	100	72	25	2	54	45

Each player takes a turn rolling the dice and placing his marker on the first number that is divisible by the number he rolled. If he skips a numeral that is divisible by the number rolled, the player must go back to the beginning. The first player to get to the end of the board is the winner.

"NUMBER BASEBALL"   Using multiplication problems from your child's text and workbooks, play the game of "Number Baseball." Easy problems at the beginning of his book count as a single, more complex problems count as doubles and triples, and the most difficult problems, when done correctly, are home runs. Any problem done incorrectly counts as one out.

The "pitcher" is the player who presents the problem to the "batter." The "pitcher" also states what kind of hit the problem is worth. After a hitter gets three outs, the players reverse roles. The game continues for nine innings, and the player with the most runs at the end of the game is the winner.

Draw a diamond on a piece of paper or cardboard and use markers to represent the batter. Pictures from the sports section of your local paper and bubble gum baseball cards serve as good markers.

"THE GREATEST OF ALL FRACTIONS"   Have your child make up 50 fraction cards with one fraction on each card. The cards are dealt to the players. Without looking, each player turns over one of his cards. The player with the fraction that has the greatest value wins that trick. The player with the most cards at the end of the game wins.

This same game can be played with decimals also.

PRACTICE IN ESTIMATING   Give your child addition problems that he must complete within ten seconds and be reasonably close to the actual answer. Remind him that the easiest way to do this is to round off the number to the nearest ten or hundreds.

EXAMPLES: 79 + 22 is easily rounded to 80 + 20, which gives a close estimate of 100; the actual answer is 101.

231 + 589 is easily rounded to 200 + 600, which gives a close estimate of 800; the actual answer is 820.

Have your child use the sales slip from the grocery bill to estimate the total by rounding off each item to the nearest dollar.

Have your child estimate the weight of each family member and then check to see how close his estimates are. Each family member can estimate the weight of ten different household items and then check the actual weight to see who is the closest.

With a map of the United States or of your state use the scale provided on the map's legend to estimate the distances from your home to ten other places without the use of a ruler. Write down your estimates and then check them by using a ruler.

Using pint, quart, and gallon containers, estimate how many containers will be filled when you let the water run for ten seconds, for thirty seconds, and so on. Change the force of the water flow and see what happens. Does your estimate get closer to the real time?

Walk a straight line for fifteen seconds. Estimate the number of yards, feet, inches you have walked, and then measure the distance.

As you drive, use the car odometer to measure the distance in miles. Tell the whole family when the mile begins and have them try to guess when the car has covered the distance.

How long will it take to walk or jog a mile? Take your child to the local quarter-mile track and jog it with him to give him a true feeling of the length of a mile. Estimate how long it will take you to jog or walk the mile.

"MONEY, MONEY, MONEY"   Make a list of dollar and cent amounts and have your child figure out the fewest bills and coins it would take to make each amount.

EXAMPLE: $ .25 (one quarter.)
$ .30 (one quarter, one nickel.)

$ .04 (four pennies.)

$ .20 (two dimes.)

$ .05 (one nickel.)

$ .48 (one quarter, two dimes, three pennies.)

$ 1.34 (one dollar, one quarter, one nickel, four pennies.)

$ 52.00 (one fifty-dollar bill, one two-dollar bill.)

$ 138.00 (one one-hundred-dollar bill, one twenty-dollar bill, one ten, one five, and three one-dollar bills.)

$2,455.00 (two one-thousand-dollar bills, four one-hundreds, one fifty, and one five-dollar bill.)

MEASUREMENT BOOK   Have your child keep a record book involving measurement. Some activities that he can record in the book follow:

Have him measure his height, arm length, waist and chest in yards, feet, inches, half inches, and quarter inches.

Using a thermometer, have him measure the temperature of ordinary tap water, of tap water with one ice cube added, with five ice cubes added. Have him measure the temperature after the water has been heated for one minute, for three minutes, when it is left at room temperature for a half hour. Have him measure the temperature of ice water after it has been left for a while in different kinds of containers (glass, styrofoam, plastic). What is the temperature when salt is added to the water?

Using graph paper, have your child use room measurements to make a scale drawing of the rooms of your house or apartment. In making a scale drawing, he should first measure all the rooms, then decide on a scale and list it in the corner of the graph paper (for example, Scale: ⅛ inch equals 1 foot). Only then should he proceed to make his drawing. You can also give your child a scale drawing of a room and have him figure out the answers to questions based on the scale. Some questions might be

How wide is the room?

How long is the room?

How wide are the windows and doors?

What is the perimeter of the room in inches, feet, and yards?

Fifth Grade

In the fifth grade, children generally learn to read and write numbers in the millions. They learn to round numbers to the nearest hundred thousand and work with the decimal system through the thousandths. They round numbers in the decimal form to the nearest whole number, and the relationship between the decimal system and the dollars and cents system is examined.

Children add and subtract numbers in the hundred thousands and the dollars and cents system. Multiplication is extended so that children can multiply any number. Division involves dividend numbers in the thousands and divisors from 10 to 99. Both multiplication and division are used to solve problems involving money.

Fifth-graders learn to express a whole number as a fraction (8/4) and a mixed number (5¾) as an improper fraction ($^{23}/_4$). They also learn to add and subtract fractional numbers and to multiply any two fractional numbers by finding the least common denominator (2/4, 4/8, 5/12 — LCD equals 4, the lowest number that can be divided into each of the three denominators evenly).

The study of time includes decades and centuries, and children continue their examination of liquid measurement. Graphing becomes more involved as children work with reading, interpreting, and constructing bar and line graphs.

The metric system, the worldwide system of measurement, is usually examined in depth in this grade (see pages 110-117).

Study of geometry includes work with plane figures such as the elipse, pentagon, and parallelogram; the classification of various angles; and the concept of area.

"GOING ON VACATION"   Give your child a road map of the United States or the state in which you live. Have your child take an imaginary vacation from your hometown to a specific destination. Give him questions such as

> What is the distance between our house and our destination? (He can figure out these distances by using the scale of miles on the map.)
>
> What is the total distance we will travel?
>
> If we take three side trips to _____ (pick out the names of three places along the route), what will be the total distance traveled?

If gasoline costs sixty cents a gallon and our car gets eighteen miles to the gallon, how much money will we have to spend on gasoline?

Our gas tank holds seventeen gallons of gasoline. How many times will we have to fill it up?

How fast can we get there if we drive an average of fifty-five miles per hour without stopping? if we take breakfast, lunch, and dinner breaks of an hour each? if we take the eating breaks as well as sleeping in motels for eight hours a night?

SHAPES AND PERIMETERS   On a sheet of paper draw different shapes and indicate the lengths of the sides of each shape. Have your child name the shape and find the perimeter. Remind him that to find the perimeter, we add the length of each of the sides.

EXAMPLES:

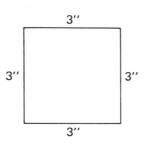

Square
perimeter = 12 inches

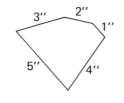

Triangle
perimeter = $5\frac{1}{2}$ "

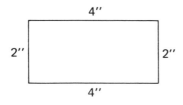

Rectangle
perimeter = 12 inches

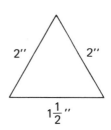

Pentagon
perimeter = 15 inches

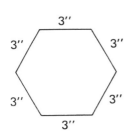

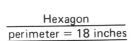

Hexagon
perimeter = 18 inches

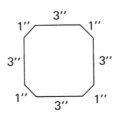

Octagon
perimeter = 16 inches

"LAST ONE OUT IS IT!"   Using markers such as buttons, pebbles, dried beans, or toothpicks, arrange them into three rows of equal amounts. (The rows may contain as many objects as you wish.) The two players take turns removing any number of objects from one row only. Any number or even the whole row may be taken by either player. The player who is forced to take the last object is the loser.

This game, which appears to be very simple, actually takes a great deal of strategy and cunning, and will give your child mental exercise in number patterns.

THE WORDS OF MATH   Throughout his study of math your child will be introduced to a mathematics vocabulary. It is important that he understand these words for work with word problems. Write the words in a column on one side of the page and have him circle that part of the problem on the right side of the page that illustrates the word.

EXAMPLES: *sum*

$$52 \\ +37 \\ \hline \widehat{89}$$

addend

$$\widehat{32} \\ +\widehat{47} \\ \hline 79$$

difference

$$97 \\ -37 \\ \hline \widehat{60}$$

subtrahend

$$48 \\ -\widehat{27} \\ \hline 21$$

minuend

$$\widehat{59} \\ -42 \\ \hline 17$$

multiplicand

$$\widehat{7} \\ \times 5 \\ \hline 35$$

product	9	*quotient*	$\boxed{3}$
	$\times 4$		$3\overline{)9}$
	$\boxed{36}$	*dividend*	3
multiplier	8		$4\overline{)\boxed{12}}$
	$\boxed{\times 8}$	*numerator*	$\boxed{4}\overline{)7}$
	64	*denominator*	$6\boxed{\overline{)9}}$
exponent	$4^{\boxed{3}}=4\times4\times4=64$	*proper fraction*	$\boxed{2/4}$, $4/2$
divisor	5	*improper fraction*	$1/2$, $\boxed{2/1}$
	$\boxed{7}\overline{)35}$	*mixed numeral*	4, $\boxed{4\frac{1}{4}}$, $2/5$

"GEO-BOARD"   Help your child construct his own geo-board. On a piece of plywood about three quarters of an inch thick and approximately one foot by one foot, have him hammer finishing nails (nails with no head at the top) so that each nail stands about one inch high and is one inch away from its neighbors. The nails should be uniformly spaced one inch apart. Most geo-boards contain eleven columns and eleven rows, thus giving an array of 100 squares. By drawing lines with a ruler, your child will be better able to make straight columns and rows of nails. With rubber bands of different colors the child can make an infinite number of designs and figures on his geo-board.

The geo-board allows children to visualize abstract math concepts and discover numerical relations and operations by themselves. Geo-boards can be used by children of all ages.

1. Have your child make his own designs. Help him record these designs on dotted paper, with the dots representing the nails on the board.

2. Make designs on dotted paper and have your child make the same designs on his geo-board.

3. Have your child practice shapes by making different sized squares, triangles, and rectangles on his board.

4. Have your child make figures that contain a specific number of nails within them. Give him problems such as

Make a triangle with five nails inside it.

Make a five-sided figure with ten nails inside it.

Make a square with sixteen nails inside it.

Make three rectangles, each having six nails inside them.

5. Have your child make different shaped figures with the same number of sides.

EXAMPLE: Different shapes of four sides

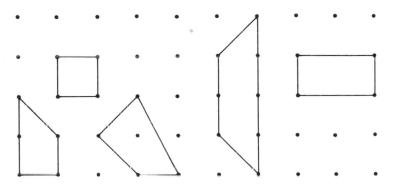

6. *Parallel Lines.* Fill your child's geo-board with different line segments so that some of them are parallel and others are not. Have him take off the rubber bands so that only parallel lines remain. Remind your child that although parallel lines remain the same distance apart at every point, they do not have to be the same length as each other.

7. *Perpendicular Lines.* Fill your child's board with intersecting lines so that some are perpendicular and others are not. Have him take off the rubber bands so that only perpendicular lines remain. Explain to your child that perpendicular lines are lines that form a right angle (square corner) when they meet.

8. Have your child make different sized figures on his geo-board and then find the perimeter of the figures with a ruler.

9. For practice in area have your child construct figures with specified areas.

EXAMPLE: Form a rectangle whose area is twelve square inches. (The area of a rectangle equals length times width.) The child, with the help of his ruler, should make a figure that looks like the following. (It could also be 12″ × 1″ or 6″ × 2″.)

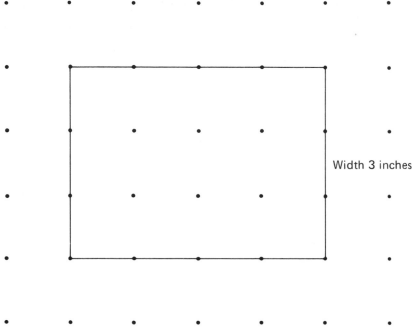

Length 4 inches

Width 3 inches

10. If your child has learned the different kinds of triangles, have him practice making shapes with them on his board.

Right triangle—one angle of the triangle is a right angle (90 degrees).

Acute triangle—all angles of the triangle are less than 90 degrees.

Obtuse triangle—one of the angles of the triangle is greater than 90 degrees.

Isosceles triangle—at least two sides of the triangle are equal in length.

Scalene triangle—no sides of the triangle are equal in length.

Equilateral triangle — all sides of the triangle are equal in length.

"HOW MUCH MONEY?" Have your child make up his own blank checks on three-by-five index cards, including the check number, date, name of bank, whom the check is being paid to, the amount, and places for his signature and for a memo of what the check is for.

EXAMPLE:

```
Ocean Bank
1771 So. St.                    check # _____
Heretown, U.S.A.
                                   date _____


        Pay to the order of _____


        _____ dollars    $ _____


    Memo: _____         _____
```

Give him problems such as:

Your monthly take-home pay is $1,000.00. You deposit $200.00 in your savings account, and you keep $250.00 for spending money. You deposit the rest of your money in your checking account, which has a balance of $197.00 from the previous month. In addition to this deposit you also deposit a birthday present of $25.00 from your Uncle Tom and Aunt Julia as well as your federal income tax refund of $137.94.

1. How much money did you deposit in your checking account from your monthly take-home pay?
2. What is your balance after you made the deposits?
3. Your bills for this month are

$250.00 rent, payable to Allhouse Management

$ 60.25, to Master Charge

$125.17 insurance bill for your car

$ 50.00 wedding present to Mr. and Mrs. Russo

$200.00 payment to Wilson National Bank for your car

$230.00 for a new stereo to Sam Goody's

Write out checks for payment of your bills and figure out your checking-account balance as you do so.

Sixth Grade

In the sixth grade, children find sums of two or more addends in the millions and also work in the millions with subtraction. They work with three-digit numerals in multiplication and division as well as dividing fractional numbers.

Ratio, percent, the decimal system through ten-thousandths, multiplication and division of numbers in decimal form, expression of fractional numbers in decimal form, and the sum and difference of fractional numbers in decimal form are learned. The relationships between fractions, decimal fractions, and percentages are also examined.

Their studies in geometry include learning the properties of regular polygons (any closed figure formed by straight lines), trapezoids, and rhombuses, as well as the concepts of perpendicular lines in a plane, lines intersecting a plane, lines parallel to a plane, and lines perpendicular to a plane. Linear measurement includes circumference of a circle. Areas of rectangular regions are examined, and the protractor is used to draw and measure angles.

Statistics and probability are examined through graphs, scale drawings, tossing dice, and comparing experimental results with theoretical probability.

"SHAKE IT, SPILL IT" Make a number board on a piι ⌐e of construction paper or cardboard by drawing lines down and across so that there are twenty squares on the board. Write any number between 10 and 100 in each square. Put three dice in a tin or plastic container. The players take turns shaking the dice and spilling them on the board. The numbers that show on the dice are used in combination with the numbers on the board that the dice land on for practice in multiplication, division, subtraction, or addition, depending on how the game is being played.

EXAMPLE:

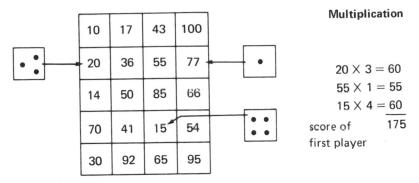

Multiplication

$20 \times 3 = 60$
$55 \times 1 = 55$
$15 \times 4 = \underline{60}$

score of   175
first player

If the game is being used for practice in multiplication, and one die showing the number 3 lands on a square showing the number 20, the player would multiply 20 times 3 and get 60 as one of his answers. The same is done with the other two dice, and the three products are added together to get the score of the first play. After ten rounds the player with the highest total is the winner.

PRACTICE WITH FRACTIONS   Explain to your child that the denominator in a fraction tells how many pieces make up the whole group or object and that the numerator tells how many of these pieces are had. Give him factual questions that he must place in fractional form.

EXAMPLES:
"One pint is what part of a quart?" (1/2)
"Two quarts are what part of a gallon?" (2/4 or 1/2)
"Three eggs are what part of a dozen?" (3/12 or 1/4)
"Three ounces are what part of a pound?" (3/16)
"Eight hours are what part of a day?" (8/24 or 1/3)
"Five months are what part of a year?" (5/12)
"Seven weeks are what part of a year?" (7/52)
"Sixty days are what part of a year?" (60/365 or 12/73)
"Eighteen cents is what part of a dollar?" (18/100 or 9/50)
"Five hundred feet are what part of a mile?" (500/5280 or 25/264)

"MANCALA"—THE AFRICAN GAME   This math game, which may very well be the world's oldest game, can be purchased in department stores or can be played with an egg carton and forty-eight counters (beans, pebbles, buttons, etc.). It will give your child practice in number patterns.

Each player has the six cups on one side of the egg carton; this constitutes his "side." At the start of the game each cup is filled with 4 counters. Each player takes his turn by taking all the counters from any one of his cups and, moving clockwise, dropping one object in each cup as he passes over it. Whenever a player drops his last counter in an empty cup, he takes all the objects in the opposite cup. It does not matter if it is his cup or if it belongs to his opponent, as long as the cup is empty.

The game ends when there are no more objects left in the egg carton or when a player has no more objects on his side to move. The player with the most objects at the end of the game is the winner.

"TENNIS LOVE"   To give your child practice in number relationships as well as practice in concentration skills, play a game of verbal tennis. The "server" (the player who begins the game) calls out any number and then immediately begins the count with the number 1. The other player counts 2, and the two players take turns alternating the count (similar to the familiar game "Buzz"). Whenever a number is to be called that either contains a number that the server called or is a multiple of that number, the player calls out "love" in place of that number. The count continues until one player makes a mistake.

The players take turns being the "server," and the first player to win four points wins the game.

> EXAMPLE: The Server (S) calls out "3 — love" to the Player (P), and the game begins.
>
> S =   1
> P =   2
> S =   love (3)
> P =   4
> S =   5
> P =   love (6 is a multiple of 3)
> S =   7
> P =   8
> S =   love (9 is a multiple of 3)
> S =   10
> P =   11

S =   love (12 is a multiple of 3)
P =   love (13 has 3 in it)
S =   14
       etc.

The first player to make a mistake by calling out a number that is a multiple of 3 or contains 3 in it (instead of saying "love") loses the point.

GRAPHS   Many children enjoy working with graphs because of their "puzzle-like" nature. Make up a line graph and ask your child questions that he must answer from reading the graph.

EXAMPLES: "What was the number of boys and girls involved in extracurricular sports activities from 1965 to 1975?" (Note: This and the following graphs in this section do not contain factual information. Parents can use almanacs and encyclopedias to find such information.)

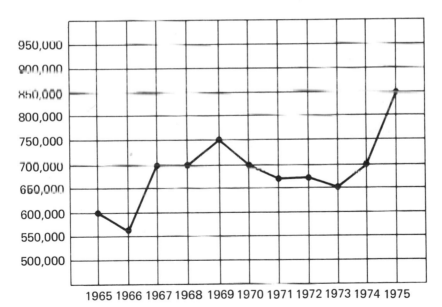

Some related questions might be

"Which year had the greatest number of children involved?"
"Which year had the least number involved?"

"Which year had 560,000 children involved?"

"What was the number of bicycles sold throughout the United States between 1970 and 1977?"

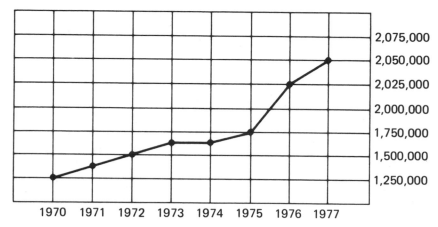

Some related questions might be

"Which year showed the highest sales?"

"Which year showed the lowest sales?"

"Which year showed the largest gain from the previous year?"

"How many bicycles were sold in 1976?"

Circle graphs are another type of graph that your child will learn in school. Have him make circle graphs of his school schedule, the ways he spends his allowance, his interests in hobbies and sports, and so on.

EXAMPLE: "Draw a circle graph showing Richard's daily schedule."

Some related questions might be

"How many hours each day does Richard spend sleeping?"

"What percentage of each day does he spend doing his homework?"

"Does he spend more time with television and sports than with dinner and homework?"

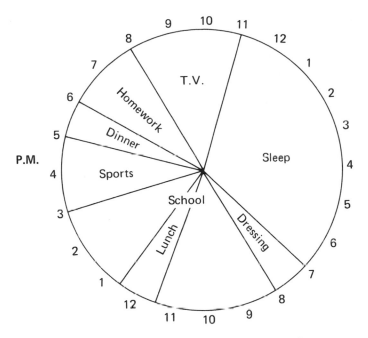

How do American teen-agers spend their money?

Money spent from each dollar

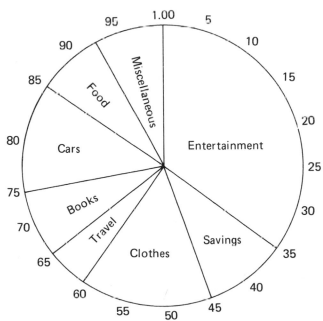

Some related questions might be

> "How much money do teen-agers spend on clothes? on food?"
>
> "What do they spend the least on?"
>
> "Is more money spent on entertainment or on miscellaneous?"

STOCKS   Using the stock listings on the financial page of the newspaper, review with your child the meanings of the different columns showing the high and low of the stock as well as the closing price.

Give stock problems to your child such as

> "I have spent $2,300.00 on International Paper stock. I have thirty-eight shares of stock. How much was each share?"
>
> "If I want to purchase seventy-two shares of IBM stock at $267.00 per share, how much money do I need?"
>
> "I bought seventy-five shares of CBS stock at $58.00 a share. It has now risen to 60½. If I sell the seventy-five shares, how much profit will I make? Deduct the broker's fee of $50.74. If my goal is to make a profit of $225.00, at what point should I sell the stock?"

Have your child choose ten different stocks and keep track of them for a number of weeks. Have him keep line graphs of the rise and fall of his stocks. Give him a hypothetical problem.

> EXAMPLE: "You won $5,000.00 in the state lottery. You decide to use this money to invest in the stock market. Using the listings from today's paper, purchase ten different stocks that you will sell in exactly four weeks from today. Figure the broker's fee at 5 percent. Keep a line graph of the rise and fall of these stocks for the next four weeks. At the end of four weeks determine your profit or loss. You could have put this money in the bank at 6 percent interest. If you had put it in the bank, would you have made more money or less? Compare the graph of your stocks with the graph of the market index (shown in the newspaper) to see if your stocks parallel the market or have gone against the trend of the market."

Give your child a graph such as the following and have him answer your questions by consulting the graph:

The Trend of a Stock over a Twelve-Month Period

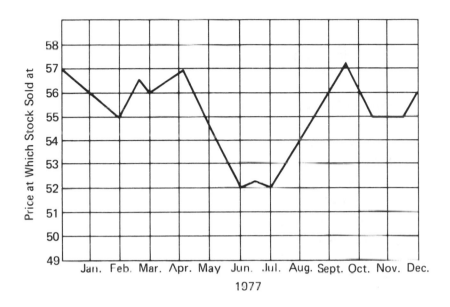

What was the highest price the stock sold at? During what month?

What was the lowest price the stock sold at? During what month?

If you had bought one hundred shares on February 1 and sold them on October 1, what profit would you have made?

If you had bought on January 1 and sold on June 1, would you have gained or lost? How much?

What average price did the stock sell at for the twelve months?

You made a "killing" on your investments. What month did you buy and what month did you sell?

What months showed the greatest decline? The greatest up-swing?

CALCULATORS Once children have a firm grasp on the concept of number and on the basic operations, a fascinating gift that can provide many hours of entertainment and self-instruction in working with numbers is a calculator. There are over fifty companies that manufacture calculators. They can be purchased at reasonable cost (five- to ten-dollar calculators are suitable for elementary school children) and can be used with children of all ages in many different ways.

Some helpful hints in using the calculator with your child are

> Get him into the habit of always checking the display as he enters each number on the machine so as to eliminate input errors, caused by pressing the wrong button.

> As you introduce your child to the uses of the calculator, teach only one function at a time.

> Don't allow your child to use the calculator to replace computation skills that he must memorize for efficiency in math (the times tables, for example).

> Have your child use the calculator to encourage thinking, not to replace it.

Calculators can be used by children of all ages. Parents should use the following games and activities as reference points only, using numbers and problems that the child is familiar with from what he has learned about math in school.

"MIND VERSUS MACHINE" To give your child practice in the basic facts of different math operations, play the following game: One player calls out a basic math problem such as "seven times eight" and, using the calculator, must show the answer on the machine before the other player, without a calculator, states the answer verbally or writes the answer on paper.

Besides giving your child practice in basic math facts, it will show him that answers to basic math facts can usually be done quicker in one's head than with a calculator.

"WHAT NUMBER AM I?" The child must find the product, quotient, sum, or difference of a problem stated by the parent.

EXAMPLE: "I am the product of 5.34 and 24.
What number am I?"

"I am the sum of 75, 7.65, 8.3, and 27.
What number am I?"

"I am the quotient of 9.50 and 17.
What number am I?"

"I am the difference between 1,876,500 and 425,389.
What number am I?"

WORD PROBLEMS Give your child word problems to solve using the calculator.

EXAMPLES: "The Sun is 93,000,000 miles away from Earth. If a rocket was sent to the Sun that traveled 1,800 miles an hour, how long would it take to reach its destination?"

"The population of the United States is 220,000,000 people. Of these people, 84 percent like pizza. How many Americans do not like pizza?"

"The number of hamburgers sold in one day was 17,553. This sale was 20 percent more than the average daily sale of hamburgers. How many hamburgers are usually sold in one day?"

CALCULATING AREA Give your child a graphic design consisting of triangles, squares, and rectangles, with labeled sides, and have him figure out the area of these shapes with his calculator.

EXAMPLE:

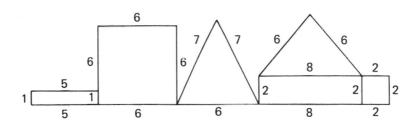

Area of a triangle equals one half the base times the height.
Area of a square equals side times side, or sides squared.
Area of a rectangle equals the length times the width.

ROUNDING NUMBERS   Give your child exercises in rounding off numbers.

EXAMPLES: Round off the following numbers to the nearest 10:

47 (50)	256 (260)
88 (90)	784 (780)
63 (60)	651 (650)
72 (70)	439 (440)

Round off the following numbers to the nearest 100:

527 (500)	1,987 (2,000)
798 (800)	2,543 (2,500)
463 (500)	9,544 (9,500)
829 (800)	6,758 (6,800)

Round off the following numbers to the nearest 1,000:

3,768 (4,000)	65,219 (65,000)
7,864 (8,000)	90,432 (90,000)
1,924 (2,000)	16,503 (17,000)
5,389 (5,000)	78,459 (78,000)

The Metric System

By an act of Congress in 1866, the metric system became the legal system of measure in the United States. Engineers and scientists realized the advantages of this system over the English system, adopted it, and have used it almost exclusively since then. The general public however, continued to use the English system.

Since the passing of the Metric Conversion Act of 1975, which called for a "national policy of coordinating the increasing use of the metric system in the United States," more and more emphasis has been placed on using the metric system in our daily lives. By the end of 1978 weather reports will be giving the temperature in degrees Celsius, the wind speed in kilometers, and the rainfall in millimeters.

In keeping with this conversion from English to metric measurements the schools are teaching the metric system as part of the math curriculum. The basic units of measure the child will encounter in school are the meter, liter, and gram. The meter (m) is the basic unit of length in the metric system and measures the same things that the yard, foot, and inch do in the English system. The gram (g) is the measurement of weight and is the counterpart of the pound and ounce in the English system. The liter (l) is the measurement of volume and is the counterpart of the gallon, quart, and pint of the English system.

Prefixes are attached to the basic metric units in order to account for decimal parts and multiples of ten of each unit. The common prefixes are

milli-	1/1000
centi-	1/100
deci-	1/10
kilo-	1000

All the units of the same measure are in multiples of ten, which makes conversions simple. This is the great advantage of the metric system over the English system. In the metric system 2,000 meters easily become 2 kilometers, whereas a conversion of 2,000 feet into miles in the English system becomes a difficult division problem (2000/5280 = 0.3789 miles).

On the prekindergarten and kindergarten level, children learn to associate the basic units with familiar objects, that is, the meter as something that is slightly taller or shorter than they are; the decimeter is as long as a worm, and a liter of water is about the same amount as two cans of soda.

In grades 1 through 3, children are introduced to the relationship of millimeters to centimeters, and meters to kilometers. Sums up to 100 are associated with the meterstick (for example, how many centimeters should be added to reach the 90 on the meterstick). The children are introduced to the Celsius thermometer, in which 0 degrees is freezing and 100 degrees is boiling, and they practice estimation with examples such as "how many liters of water do you think it will take to fill this fish tank?" They weigh classroom objects in grams and kilograms and learn that the metric ton is equivalent to 1,000 kilograms.

Fourth-, fifth-, and sixth-graders learn equivalence thoroughly: That 90 on the meterstick is the same as 97/100 meter, 9 decimeters, 90 centimeters, or 970 millimeters. Time, rate, and distance problems are taught, and the history of the system and its worldwide use are explained.

METRIC ACTIVITIES   Purchase a metric tape and meterstick from your local hardware store and have your child use them with the following activities:

1. Have him look for objects and measure distances that are the same approximate length as the meter, such as: the distance around the edge of a looseleaf sheet of paper, the width of a window or door, the length of a coffee table, a desk blotter, and so on. Then have him use his meterstick to find the difference between the length or width of these objects and a meter.

2. On large sheets of paper play the meter estimation game with the entire family. Each person draws a circle on paper. Each circle is measured with the meter tape. The individual whose circle is closest to the meter length gets one point. Then have each family member toss a coin on a rug for a distance of two, three, four, or five meters. Have your child measure the distance with his meterstick. Once again, the closest toss gets one point, and the first to reach ten is the "meter king" or "meter queen".

METRIC DRAWINGS

1. Have your child draw shapes, figures, and pictures of objects, labeling the lengths and widths of their respective parts in millimeters, centimeters, and decimeters.

1 millimeter   -

1 centimeter   ——

1 decimeter   ——————————————————————————————

2. Have your child keep graph measurements of his height in millimeters, centimeters, decimeters, and meters.

3. Give your child instructions such as, "Draw a ten-sided figure with sides that are of the following measurements:

> ten millimeters, five centimeters, two decimeters, five millimeters, three centimeters, one decimeter, one millimeter, ten centimeters, three decimeters, and twenty-five millimeters."

VERBAL GUESSING GAMES   Describe something using metric specifications and have your child guess what it is.

> EXAMPLES: "The insect I am thinking of is only one or two millimeters long. What is it?" (An ant.)

> "This animal has a neck about three meters long. What is it?" (A giraffe.)

"Name a bird that is about one decimeter long." (A sparrow.)

"This animal has a nose that is two or three meters long. What is it? (An elephant.)

MILLIMETERS   To give your child practice in estimating and measuring millimeters (the smallest metric-scale unit), give him items such as paper clips, pins, pens, pencils, coins, buttons, books, forks, spoons, material, and so on. Have him draw a picture of the item, write down his estimate, and then write down the true measurement. This same exercise can be done with sets of things, such as sets of different sized nails, sets of buttons, different sized pieces of paper, lengths of string, different sized rocks or twigs, or by simply drawing lines of different lengths on a page. (Obviously, all the above exercises can be done to provide reinforcement in the centimeter and decimeter as well.)

CELSIUS TEMPERATURE   Explain to your child that in the metric system the everyday measurement of temperature is the degree Celsius. The word *Celsius* means the same as *Centigrade*. The boiling point of water is 100 degrees C and the freezing point is 0 degrees C. Normal human body temperature in metric is 37 degrees C. This corresponds to 98.4 degrees F.

One person fills a cup with different blends of hot and cold water. Each player guesses what the temperature is and then checks it with a thermometer.

WEIGHT   Explain to your child that the unit of weight in the metric system is the gram. Just as with the meter, the gram is broken into parts that are smaller than it and is used to make up new quantities that are larger than it.

Milligram means 1/1000 gram (1,000 mg = 1 g).

Centigram means 1/100 gram (100 cg = 1 g).

Decigram means 1/10 gram (10 dg = 1 g).

Decagram means 10 grams (1 dag = 10 g).

Hectogram means 100 grams (1 hg = 100 g).

Kilogram means 1,000 grams (1 kg = 1,000 g).

A paper clip weighs approximately one gram. Have your child make a list and illustrate with drawings other things that he can think of that could weigh approximately one gram. Some of these things might be a fly, a safety pin, a leaf, a piece of paper, a drop of water, a tissue, a lady bug, a butterfly.

Your child can make a coat-hanger balance by puncturing two aluminum pans and threading string through the holes, then attaching the end of each string to a wire hanger. By using a paper clip (1 gram), a sugar cube (2 grams), or a nickel (5 grams), as a balancing weight in one pan, he can discover the approximate weight of objects by placing them in the other pan. The coat-hanger balance would look like this:

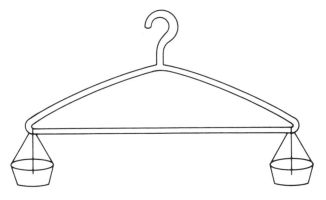

Buy your child a metric scale to weigh himself and have him keep graphs of his weight. Weigh household items by having each family member guess the weight and then check to see who is the closest.

THE LITER   Explain to your child that a liter is a little more than a quart. In the metric system volume is measured in liters. The prefixes are the same as they are for measures of weight and length.

  1,000 milliliters equal 1 liter.

  100 centiliters equal 1 liter.

  10 deciliters equal 1 liter.

  1 decaliter is equal to 10 liters.

  1 hectoliter is equal to 100 liters.

  1 kiloliter is equal to 1,000 liters.

Obtain a liter container for your child to use in his experiments. Many different wines come in bottles the size of a liter. Have your child do estimation exercises to find out

How many juice cans of water make up a liter?

How many glasses of water make up a liter?

How much more does a liter hold than a quart?

How many liters will he get from a bucket of water?

A METRIC VACATION IN KILOMETERS   Give your child problems in linear measurement.

EXAMPLE: The marathon race lasted about five hours. The winner was a young man named John Smith. Study his route and answer the questions.

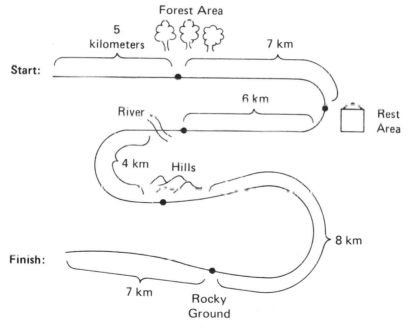

How many kilometers did John run?

When he reached the river how many more kilometers did he have to run to finish the race?

How many kilometers did he travel between the forest area and the rocky ground area?

When he reached the hills, what percentage of the race had he completed? What percentage did he still have to run?

METRIC PERIMETERS   Give your child activities in finding perimeter in metric units.

EXAMPLE: Find the perimeter of each figure in centimeters. Use your metric ruler. Then find the perimeter in millimeters.

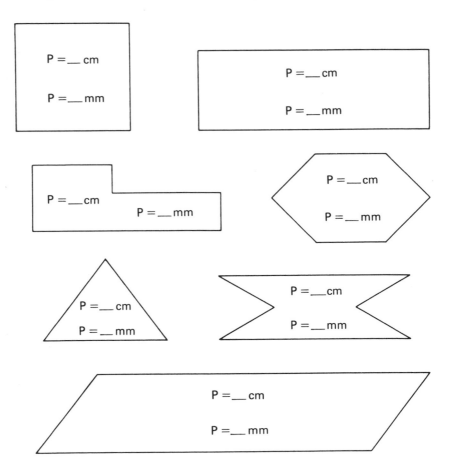

NOTE: All the math activities that deal with measurement in the English system throughout the math section can be used by parents to reinforce the child's understanding of the metric system.

The process of learning mathematics is an experience in logical inquiry. The elementary school math curriculum encourages this logical inquiry by having children use their minds in understanding the various mathematical aspects of the world. In short, it seeks to develop the natural curiosity of children. Encourage his curiosity and your child will always want to learn.

6

Social Studies

Each school district has a somewhat different approach to the teaching of social studies. However, almost every social studies curriculum has common elements, and from these a basic outline can be prepared for parents who wish to reinforce their children's school learning in the home.

It is important for parents to go beyond the curriculum outline in this chapter by getting to know the specific topics and ideas the school is teaching the child. This can easily be done by talking to your child's teacher and by looking over your child's social studies textbook and his homework assignments.

Learning About the World

The following is a brief summary of the basic elements common to most social studies curriculum guides.

HISTORY   The child learns that history is a continuous process leading to the present; that human beings are a product of their past; that every event, movement, and institution has roots in the past. The customs, traditions, values, and beliefs of the present have been passed from generation to generation. The child learns that events have multiple causes and effects, how historians acquire their information—from written records, artifacts, and oral traditions—and how each generation must rediscover, verify, and explain the past for itself. The child learns about change, that it is a constant in history and an inevitable condition of life and that some change has been progressive whereas other change has been detrimental.

GEOGRAPHY   The child learns about the universe, the earth, his neighborhood, and aoout how each is affected by the others. Through examining the geographic environment and its resources he comes to understand how the earth changes human beings and human beings change the earth. He learns how geographic factors have a significant role in the livelihood of a nation, how climate affects production, and how nations have adapted themselves to their specific climates. The child uses maps and globes to understand the geography of the world. He learns how technology has affected man's development.

ECONOMICS   The child learns that human wants consist of materials, goods, and services; that the economic wants of society are never completely satisfied; and that the conservation of natural resources is necessary in order to fulfill these human wants. Decision about how to use limited resources is the basis of every economic system, and the child learns how such decisions created the various economic systems of capitalism, socialism, and communism. From this study the child learns how every society must choose what goods and services it will produce and how increased productivity makes possible the greater satisfaction of human wants. Production of goods and services becomes more efficient through specialization and the division of labor.

Through an examination of the American economy today, the child learns how consumers, producers, and government interrelate.

POLITICAL SCIENCE   Children study the various forms of government (with particular emphasis on our democratic form of government) and how those governments make rules for group living. They learn the principles of our society: that ultimate power resides in the people and that people have certain inalienable rights. They also learn how government officials are elected and how federal, state, and local governments operate.

ANTHROPOLOGY-SOCIOLOGY   Children learn about the various races of the world, the basic needs of all humans, and the different cultures and environments and how they affect people. They learn that human beings are much more alike than they are different and that people are social creatures who live in groups for the benefit of the individual as well as the group.

The various areas of the social studies curriculum provide the child with a strong foundation for understanding the world in which he lives. The following activities are based on the concepts studied in these areas and are grouped according to grade level, from prekindergarten through sixth grade. Although these activities are based on the typical learning activities of the grade level, parents should realize that many of the activities listed for each grade can be used for the other grades as well.

Prekindergarten and Kindergarten

On this level children learn about the classroom, the teacher, the purpose for school, and about elementary rules and regulations concerning daily routines, working together, and sharing with others.

They are introduced to the concepts of the family and of community workers through storybooks, dressing up in costumes, film strips, and songs. They learn about the weather and how it affects what we do, that certain days are special days and that some people and places are near and some are far away.

TRIPS   As the old saying states, "A picture is worth a thousand words." One of the best ways that children learn is by visiting places such as the supermarket, department stores, fire and police stations, and other areas of interest in the local neighborhood. Such trips are fun and exciting and enable the young child to see, feel, hear, smell, touch, and sometimes taste what is going on. So, as you take care of your daily responsibilities that entail walks through the neighborhood, remember that such an experience can be a true learning experience for your child when the neighborhood, like the home, is used as a classroom. Are you going to the store to buy some milk? Discuss with him where milk comes from, what cows eat, how trucks carry the containers to the store, and how we work to earn money so we can pay for the milk we need to be healthy. Do this with other shops you visit and you will be providing your child with a wealth of information that will help him succeed in school.

The amount of knowledge children acquire on trips, however, is greatly influenced by the readiness activities that are presented to them before the actual trip takes place. One of the best pretrip activities for any child is the reading together of books about what the child is about to experience, followed by a discussion of the subject matter. Such books can be borrowed from the library. (See bibliography for listings of such books or ask your librarian for her suggestions.)

DISCARDED ADULT CLOTHES   Children of this age love to dress like adults. A box of old clothes and shoes provides many hours of enjoyable learning experiences as children develop their imagination, creativity, and language by pretending that they are adults. The box can include old hats, ties, shoes, jackets, dresses, gloves, coats, and belts.

CUTOUTS   Using old books, magazines, and newspapers, have the child cut out pictures of family members—mother, father, boys and girls, babies. The child can make a booklet with the title page labeled "The Family" by pasting the pictures onto different pages. Consecutive pages might contain

> pictures of large families and small families
>
> pictures of mothers
>
> pictures of fathers
>
> pictures of boys
>
> pictures of girls
>
> pictures of aunts, uncles, grandparents.

THE "WHO AM I?" GAME   The parent acts out the activities of a community worker, and the child guesses who the parent is. Then the child acts out the activities, and the parent must guess.

SONGS   Through songs children learn about themselves, the world, people, places, and things.

1. The wheels on the bus go round,   (Hands go around
     round, round;   and around.)
   Round, round, round; round,
     round, round;
   The wheels on the bus go round,
     round, round—
   All around the town.

The horn on the bus goes beep,
  beep, beep;
Beep, beep, beep; beep, beep,
  beep;
The horn on the bus goes beep,
  beep, beep—
All around the town.

(Let one hand be
  the horn and
  the other push
  it.)

The baby on the bus goes waa,
  waa, waa, waa . . .

(Hold arms as if
  cradling a
  baby.)

The mommy on the bus goes shh,
  shh, shh . . .

(Hold finger to
  lips.)

The daddy on the bus says,
  "Sit right down . . ."

(Shake finger.)

Children love to sing and act out things they do every day at home and in school. Using the tune for "Here We Go 'Round the Mulberry Bush," the children can go through all the things they do each day—washing their faces, putting on their clothes, walking to school, rolling the ball, sweeping the floor, eating dinner. A song such as the following one is a nice way to learn:

2. "This Is The Way We . . ."
  This is the way I wash my face,
  Wash my face, wash my face;
  This is the way I wash my face,
  So early in the morning.

Other verses may be as follows:

This is the way I . . .
  Eat my breakfast;
  Drink my juice;
  Brush my teeth;
  Brush my hair;

Put on my socks;
Put on my shoes;
Put on my coat;
Open the door;
Walk to school.

Here is a song for learning parts of the body and developing a good feeling about movement.

3. "Looby Lu"

Now we dance Looby Lu;
Now we dance Looby Li;
Now we dance Looby Lu;
All on a Saturday night.

I put my right hand in,
I take my right hand out,
I give my hand a shake, shake, shake,
And I turn myself around.

Other verses are as follows:

I put my . . .
    Left hand in . . .
    Two hands in . . .
    Right foot in . . .
    Left foot in . . .
    Whole self in . . .

Chorus:
Now we dance Looby Lu;
Now we dance Looby Li;
Now we dance Looby Lu;
All on a Saturday night.

When playtime is over and it is time to clean up and get ready for dinner or bed, sing this song:

4. "No More Playing"

No more playing, no more playing;
Time to clean up;

Time to clean up;
No more playing, no more playing;
Time to clean up.

The following song gives the child experience with the expression of feelings:

5. If you're happy and you know it,
   Clap your hands;
   If you're happy and you know it,
   Clap your hands;
   If you're happy and you know it,
   Then your face is going to show it;
   If you're happy and you know it,
   Clap your hands.

Here are some other verses to use, and you can add more.

If you're sad . . . wipe your eyes;

If you're mad . . . stamp your feet;

If you're sleepy . . . close your eyes;

If you're silly . . . shake your arms;

If you're thirsty . . . take a drink.

An enjoyable way for children to learn about the family and community members is with songs.

6. "Did You Ever See My Family" (sung to the tune of "Did You Ever See a Lassie")
   Did you ever see my father, my father, my father,
   Did you ever see my father?
   A carpenter is he.
   Go this way and that way,
   Go this way and that way,
   Did you ever see my father?
   A carpenter is he.

(Substitute *mother, aunt, uncle, brother, sister, baby, grandparents, cousins,* and appropriate activities.)

7. "Everybody Do This"
   Everybody do this,
   Do this, do this
   Everybody do this
   Just like a *Fireman*.

(Child imitates such actions of a fireman as climbing a ladder or holding a hose to put out a fire. Parent follows the action of the child.)

8. "Johnny Has One Friend"
   Johnny has one friend,
   One friend, one friend.
   Johnny has one friend,
   He's the policeman.

   Johnny has two friends,
   Two friends, two friends.
   Johnny has two friends,
   The policeman and fireman.

(Substitute names of other family members and use other kinds of community workers as additional friends.)
   Other appropriate songs are

"Old MacDonald"	"Billy Boy"
"Mr. Policeman"	"Hanukkah"
"Over the River"	"London Bridge"
"Yankee Doodle"	"Farmer in the Dell"
"Little Shoemaker"	"This Old Man"

These and many other songs can be found in such books as

The Fireside Book of Children's Songs, collected and edited by Marie Winn, musical arrangement by Allan Miller, illustrated by John Alcorn (Simon and Schuster, 1966).

More Songs to Grow On, by Beatrice Landeck, drawings by David Stone Martin, arrangements by Florence White (William Sloane Assoc., 1954).

Complete Nursery Song Book, by Inez Bertail, illustrated by Walt Kelly (Lothrop, Lee and Shepard, 1967).

"WHO MADE IT?" To help your child become aware that certain things in our world are made by man and other things are made by nature without man's influence, have him leaf through magazines and newspapers and cut out pictures of things that are made by man (cars, planes, machines, clothes, tools, etc.) and pictures of things that are made by nature (flowers, trees, the sun, rivers, rocks and soil, etc.).

He can paste these pictures into separate booklets or keep them in separate envelopes.

Make use of the pictures by asking your child questions.

> EXAMPLES: "Show me something that is made by man and we use it when we visit Aunt Josephine and Uncle Frank?" (A car.)
>
> "Show me something that is made by nature and we swim in it in the summer." (A lake.)

NEIGHBORHOOD-WORKER RIDDLES   Give your child riddles concerning the activities of neighborhood workers and have him guess who the worker is.

> EXAMPLES: "He works in a white uniform. He brings us something to eat. He rings a bell to tell us he is coming." (The ice-cream man.)
>
> "He wears a blue uniform. He helps people cross the street. He carries a gun and a stick." (The policeman.)

HOLIDAYS   Children can learn about the different holidays we celebrate throughout the year by making a picture book of the symbols, foods, and activities that go along with each holiday. Such a project for Thanksgiving would include pictures of turkeys, Indians, corn, pies, the leaves turning brown, pilgrims, and a family sitting down to a Thanksgiving meal.

First and Second Grades

During these school years children are introduced to the concept of living together as a family in the community. The family meets its needs by the various community workers supplying many services to them. Families vary—sometimes a family has no father, sometimes its members change because parents leave or new babies are born or relatives come to live as part of the family. Families live in communities called neighborhoods. The communities serve the family by providing schools, fire stations, libraries, stores, police, dental and medical clinics, garbage disposal, and other services for the health and protection of the people.

The larger community of the city or town is made up of many smaller neighborhoods. Cities and towns exist all over the world. The people of the world are brought closer together through communication and transportation. The people throughout the world have the same needs for food, clothing, shelter, and work, but many of these groups have different customs, beliefs and ways of living. Children are introduced to the similarities and differences of the various nationalities throughout the world.

VISITS   Visits throughout the metropolitan area during this year will greatly reinforce the child's school learning. Take your child to city hall, banks, harbors, airports, historical sites, the court house, garment and food production centers, and museums. Find out from your local newspaper what children's social events, such as plays, fairs, carnivals, concerts, and synagogue and church gatherings, are taking place, and take the whole family.

Travel by bus, train, subway, taxi, ferryboat; visit the airport. Talk about the various modes of transportation and the specific characteristics of each.

Take a ride in the country and the city and discuss the differences between life in the country and life in the city.

Books that reinforce such visits are

Someone Always Needs a Policeman, by David Brown (Simon and Schuster, 1972), acquaints young readers with the responsibilities and duties of policemen.

What Happens When You Mail a Letter, by Arthur Shay (Reilley and Lee, 1967), describes the handling of a letter from the time it is mailed until it reaches its destination.

I Know a Grocer, by Lorraine Henriod, with illustrations by Albert Orbaan (Putnam's, 1970), is a story about two children who visit a grocery and learn how it functions for the community.

Let's Go to a Jetport, by Barbara Rich, with illustrations by Harris Petie (Putnam, 1973), describes the complex activities of the airport personnel who service and inspect the planes, control air traffic, maintain runways, and enforce customs regulations.

The Night Workers, by Alvin Schwartz, with photos by Ulli Steltzer (Dutton, 1966), is a photographic story of the fireman, policeman, baker, and other people who work at night while the rest of the city is asleep.

MAKING STORYBOOKS   Children can broaden their knowledge of topics by cutting out pictures that expand information on family and community affairs. The names of items and activities shown in the pictures should be printed on the page next to the pictures.

> EXAMPLES: "Human Development"—Consecutive pages would show
>> pictures of babies
>> pictures of young children
>> pictures of older children
>> pictures of adults
>> pictures of older adults
>
> "Specific Functions of Community Workers"—Consecutive pages would show
>> policemen as crossing guards
>> policemen as protectors of people
>> policemen giving out tickets
>> policemen giving first aid
>> policemen arresting a burglar
>
> "Foods"—Separate storybooks could be made on the various types of fruits, vegetables, meats, and liquids we consume, and where such foods come from.

SOCIAL STUDIES RIDDLES   These riddles are fun to play with children wherever you are. The parent asks

> "I need soap.
> Where do I go to get it?"
>
> "I need clothes.
> Where do I go to get them?"
>
> "I need bread.
> Where do I go?"

"I need shoes.
Where do I go?"

Reverse roles with your child, having him make up the statements. Many riddles have more than one answer. We buy shoes at shoe stores, at department stores, and sometimes at the shoemaker's shop. Encourage your child to think of all the possibilities.

LOTTO GAMES   For learning about goods and services as well as for improving the child's skills in matching, classifying, and concept building, parent and child can make lotto games. Cut out or draw pictures of workers such as farmer, baker, butcher, policeman, doctor, mailman, fireman, and so on. Paste the pictures onto one large cardboard square. Then cut out objects and goods that are a part of that individual's output or daily routine. The child picks up a picture and places it on the worker's square.

PHOTO ALBUM   As you take your child on trips throughout the neighborhood, take pictures of him in the different places you visit. Have him stand on the fire engine, have him hold a broom next to the garbage disposal truck, have him stand next to the meats in the butcher's shop or kneel in meditation at the church or synagogue. Paste the photos under captions such as "Margaret at the firehouse" and give the date. Write a few lines of the child's statements about the experience under the photo. The entire family will enjoy looking at these pictures for years and years to come.

WORKBOOKS   Have your child cut and paste, draw, or take photographs on the following themes:

"Places of Interest in the City"—skyscrapers, historic landmarks, museums, zoos, botanical gardens, subways, theaters, concert halls, statues, department stores, businesses, restaurants, parks, harbors

"How People Live in the City"—housing projects, apartment houses, brownstones, one- and two-family houses, slums, luxury apartments, hotels

"Various Nationalities in the City"—visit ethnic neighborhoods and point out the various characteristics of the people, their food, and their culture to give the child background information before he makes his booklet

FOODS OF VARIOUS NATIONALITIES   Ethnic dinner menus are great family fun and an interesting way of teaching what foods are consumed in different cities throughout the world as well as the cultures of various nationalities.

The meal can be centered around a weekly theme in which certain experiences are gained throughout the week, culminating with a Sunday meal.

EXAMPLE: For developing a theme on the French city of Paris:

Monday — Visit the library and borrow books about France as well as records of songs in the French language. A classic story about a French boy is *The Red Balloon* by Albert Lamorisse (Doubleday, 1956).

Tuesday — Read books about the French people; locate France and Paris on a map.

Wednesday — Listen to French songs. Practice simple words in the French language.

Thursday — Develop a menu of foods the French people eat.

Friday — Go shopping for the food.

Saturday — Visit an historical site or cultural museum that demonstrates some aspect of French culture.

Sunday — Make and eat the meal.

Sample menu for a French meal:
    Onion soup with cheese and bread
    Omelet or soufflé
    Green salad with homemade oil and vinegar dressing
    French bread
    Fruit and cheese for dessert

Other national dinners are

Shepherd's Pie (chopped meat and mashed potatoes) for Irish night

Lasagna (noodles, cheese, and meat sauce) for Italian night

Pork and rice for Puerto Rican night

Fish and chips (fried fish and french fries) for English night

Chili Con Carne (ground meat, kidney beans, tomato sauce, spices) for Mexican night

Consult an international cookbook for these and other dishes.

PROJECTS ON HOW THE CITY RECEIVES ITS GOODS AND SERVICES
Make a project on the needs of the city, such as water, electricity, and food, and on how the city receives these necessities.

EXAMPLE: On a large piece of cardboard or in booklet form parents can help their children make a pictorial essay from pictures, drawings, and photographs about how the city obtains its drinking water. They would show

the sun melting mountain snows, which form small streams

small streams converging into larger streams

streams converging to form rivers

a river flowing into a reservoir

large pipes carrying water from the reservoir into the city

smaller pipes taking the water from under the city streets up into our homes

the family using the water for drinking, cooking, and washing

Third and Fourth Grades

During these grades children are often introduced to the characteristics of different geographical regions, developing an understanding about living conditions in such regions as deserts, rainforests, grasslands, mountains, and northern forests. They develop insights into the ways in which people respond to the natural conditions and the variety of ethnic and cultural differences. They learn how the culture in which people live greatly influences their personalities, values, and patterns of behavior and that the basic social institutions—the family, religion, education, government—exist in all societies.

During these school years children usually learn about the American people and something of the history of our country as well. The curriculum usually begins with the study of how the Americas were discovered and explored, how the colonies were settled and developed, and how the United States was established. The contributions of some of the great leaders of America are also introduced.

THE "ME, AND HOW I GOT TO BE" BOOK   Have your child construct a photographic history of your family by accumulating pictures of family members, including as many past generations as possible. If there are missing photographs of certain family members, he and other family members can draw pictures of those persons in place of the photographs. Dates of birth and names can be placed next to the photos.

EXAMPLE: Consecutive pages would contain

> a picture of himself
> pictures of brothers and sisters
> pictures of his parents
> pictures of maternal grandparents
> pictures of paternal grandparents
> pictures of great-grandparents

The photographic history can be expanded into a family map. Using an atlas, have him trace the state in which he was born, mark off the city or town and write something such as "I was born in Lansing, Michigan, on [birth date]." He can do the same for each of his parents as well as for the country his grandparents or great-grandparents came from. Have him write factual information in his book such as

"Grandmother and Grandfather Macaluso took a boat from Italy and landed in New York in 1920."

"Mother and father lived in Virginia during World War II while father was in the navy."

"Uncle Jim moved to California and got married in 1958."

Other activities your child can do to expand his knowledge concerning his family follow:

1. Have him write letters to relatives asking them for information concerning the family and any old photographs they might have that can be included in his album.

2. When visiting relatives, he can tape-record conversations about past family occurrences and what it was like in the old days.

3. Find out the burial sites of previous-generation relatives and visit the cemetery on your next family outing.

4. Collect memorabilia such as old records, stamps, newspaper clippings, post cards, artifacts, and certificates that exemplify the times and dates of your family history.

5. Have your child read books concerning the country of your ancestors, as well as biographies of famous Americans who also came from the country of your ancestors.

6. Every group of people in the world has poems that reflect their life and history. Check your library for specific selections as well as general anthologies of verses that contain poems from many different lands and times.

7. Hundreds of family names tell a story about an ancestral occupation, birthplace, or characteristic. Have your child trace the history of your family name.

8. Borrow recordings of national songs from the library and have the child begin a study of the language of the foreign country. By practicing just a few words every day the entire family can experience the flavor of a second language.

A joint activity such as this one can be an exciting adventure into the past for the entire family, and you and your child will take great pride in it for years and years to come.

"THE FAMOUS-PEOPLE GAME"   To reinforce what the child learns in school about famous Americans, make this lotto game with your child. Borrow library books with pictures of famous Americans. Have your child use tracing paper to copy the faces of these individuals. Paste six faces each onto four cardboard squares. Cut a square of paper for each face the same size as the pictures. On each piece of paper write a few sentences about the famous American. Each player must pick a paper, read the sentences, and place it on his square if it pertains to one of his people or else replace it in the deck.

EXAMPLES:

George Washington — "I was the commander in-chief of the Revolutionary army and the first president of the United States."

Betsy Ross — "I made the first American flag."

Benjamin Franklin — "I invented many things and was the American who wrote *Poor Richard's Almanac.*"

Abraham Lincoln — "I was the sixteenth president and gave the Gettysburg Address."

Martin Luther King, Jr. — "I marched on Washington, D.C., to make my dream come true."

Pocahontas — "I was an Indian princess who helped the colonists."

John Peter Zenger — "I defended freedom of the press."

This game can be broken down into specific areas, such as people who are famous for having fought in defense of the nation (John J. Pershing, Douglas MacArthur, Dwight Eisenhower) or people who led in the fight for freedom (George Washington, Paul Revere, Abraham Lincoln, Martin Luther King, Jr.).

"CAREERS THEN AND NOW"   Have your child find out about the kinds of jobs people held in other times. For example, have him read some of the books in Leonard Everett Fisher's Colonial Americans Series, such as *The Glassmakers*, *The Hatters*, *The Papermakers*, *The Peddlers*, *The Potters*, *The Tanners*, *The Wigmakers*, and *The Schoolmakers* (Watts).

After finding out about careers in the past, children can make an in-depth study of careers today. This information will broaden their knowledge about our world as well as introduce them to the various careers so that one day they will be more competent in choosing their own. Guide this in-depth study by having him understand the entire gamut of areas that each career entails.

EXAMPLE: In introducing your child to the field of law, some activities might be

Obtain books from the library on lawyers, the laws of the country, and the lives of famous lawyers.

Discuss laws that affect the lives of citizens and the reasons why such laws are necessities.

Visit courtrooms and let your child witness a trial, explaining the various duties of lawyers, judges, juries, and witnesses.

For more information about the legal aspects of our society, parents can write to the American Bar Association, 1155 East 60th Street, Chicago, Illinois 60637 for the *Directory of Law-Related Activities*. Another volume distributed by the American Bar Association is their *Bibliography of Law-Related Curriculum Materials*.

For other careers ask the librarian for addresses of professional associations and write to them for information.

"THE WHERE DO I COME FROM? GAME"   Parent and child take turns formulating a riddle in relation to a geographic region and to the way of life in that region.

EXAMPLE: "Where I live, it is hot; there is very little water; I travel on an animal. Where do I come from and how do I travel?" (Reply: "You live in the desert, and you travel by camel.")

"Where I live it is very cold; very few things grow, and an animal pulls me. Where do I come from and how do I travel?" (Reply: "You live in the Arctic, and you travel by dogsled.")

"FAMOUS-PEOPLE CHARADES"   The child and parent take turns acting out a statement of the deeds of a famous individual by using hand, body, and motion language only. No words are allowed by the one who is trying to tell the story. The observers have to verbalize the story by guessing each word that the actor is trying to express and then name the famous person.

EXAMPLE:

I	—person points to himself
walked	—person walks around the room
on	—person places something on the table
moon	—person makes a circle with his finger and points up to the sky

(Answer: Neil Armstrong.)

MAKING MAPS   Map making usually begins in a very elementary way in the first and second grades. You can help your child understand how maps help us by proceeding slowly, making sure the child understands each step before going on to the next one.

1. With your child, make a map of each room in your house with drawings of the furniture, doors, and windows. At the bottom of the map define the symbols for the furniture, doors, and windows and label the different parts of the map with the symbols.

> EXAMPLES: *F* for furniture
> *D* for doors
> *W* for windows

2. Make a map of your own house lot or city block. Make it to scale, measuring or pacing the perimeter. Use the actual home owners' and shop names as labels.

3. Make a map of your child's route to school. Use symbols.

4. Make a map of the neighborhood.

5. Acquire a map of the city or town in which you live. With your child fill in details of particular interest.

6. Acquire a large wall map of the United States and have your child paste cut-out magazine pictures on each state depicting the main products and industries of each state.

7. Have him do the same for each country, using a map of the world.

Some sources for free or inexpensive map materials are

> your local car service station
>
> chambers of commerce (national, state, and local)
>
> state tourist information services
>
> major oil companies
>
> the state highway commission
>
> Superintendent of Documents, Government Printing Office, Washington, D.C. 20025
>
> the library (you can make photocopies)
>
> your local bookstore and variety store

GEOGRAPHIC THEME BOOKS   Have the child choose a geographic location such as the Arctic, the desert, the mountains, the rainforest, or the grasslands region and complete a thorough study of this region, including information about population, family life, how needs are secured, form of government, religion, education, language, arts, industry and agriculture, methods and modes of transportation and communication, and particular variables of the climate.

Information concerning these aspects of society can be found in the following books:

People Around the World, by Rozella Donan and Jane Hefflcfinger, with illustrations by Bernard Garbutt (Elk Grove, 1968), illuminates the differences and similarities in shelter, clothing, food, labor, and communication among the world's peoples.

The First Book Altas, by Hammond Incorporated (Watts, 1973), provides maps and statistical data concerning the geography of the United States and the rest of the world.

The Grosset World Atlas (Grosset and Dunlap, 1973), provides a collection of maps that depict the topographic features, political boundaries, and economic resources of each nation and region.

INTERESTING RESEARCH PROJECTS   In helping your child become interested in research projects that will reinforce his curriculum learning in school, use his and her playtime activities as a basis for ideas. If your children like to play with dolls, they can research the history of dolls from colonial days to the present. If they play baseball with friends on the block, get them interested in the evolution of sports from the past to the present. They can find books, trace pictures, visit museums, make models, and display their work on a shelf in their room or in the living room.

Fifth and Sixth Grades

In these grades the social studies curriculum often focuses on the economic aspects of human endeavor. Children study how various nations throughout the world use their natural resources for their development and how geography affects the economics of each country. Through this study the children discover how man uses his natural surroundings to improve his economy, and they come to understand the interrelationships among worldwide economic systems.

Current events are interwoven into the curriculum, which allows children to understand the present in relation to the past.

The beginnings and development of civilization in different areas of the world are also explored. Some of the major contributions to Western civilization of the ancient Middle East, Greece, Rome, and Medieval and Renaissance Europe are explored. Pupils become acquainted with sources of our knowledge of the past such as material remains, artifacts, oral traditions, pictorial data, and written records. They learn to draw valid conclusions and hypotheses based on evidence. They learn that the modern world owes a great debt to the past.

COLLECTING COINS AND STAMPS   The entire family can participate in developing a coin or stamp collection. Such activities enable parents to lead the child into the areas of geography and history.

Stamp collections, because of their bright colors, scenes, objects, and individuals pictured, usually have more appeal for children. Children can discover what country the stamp is from, the individual, animal, or object that is on the stamp, and the reason why it is there. A good source for a beginner's collection of stamps is the H. A. Harris Company, Boston, Massachusetts 02117. This company sends out envelopes, each containing as many as twenty packets, and customers may return all of them or keep the ones they want, returning the others along with their payment for the stamps they keep. Stamp-collecting authorities suggest that children start with used stamps and that foreign ones might make the introduction to collecting easier: one thousand such stamps can be purchased at stamp-collecting stores for less than five dollars. Have your child write letters to friends and relatives asking them to save their stamps for him.

Although foreign stamps are often the best way of getting a child interested in stamp collecting, United States pennies are great for starting a coin collection. Parents can help their child look for dates and mint marks. The mint mark, underneath the date, tells where the coin was struck; D is for Denver, S for San Francisco, and no mark means that the coin was struck in Philadelphia. Projects might include collecting Lincoln pennies for each date and mint, or Indian head pennies or nickels. Coins are more difficult and expensive for a child to collect than stamps. Coin shops sell about sixty pennies, with dates not usually found in normal circulation, for approximately ten dollars, but children can use the bank as a good source, simply exchanging the pennies they have for others from the bank teller. Some books on stamp and coin collecting are

Stamp Collector's Handbook, by Fred Reinfeld, adapted by Burton Hobson (Doubleday, 1970), contains a brief history of the United States postal system, a guide to stamp collecting, and a catalogue of U.S. issues.

Collecting Stamps, by Paul Villiard (Doubleday, 1974), contains information on handling and identifying stamps and recognizing symbols and distinguishing marks.

Catalogue of the World's Most Popular Coins, by Fred Reinfeld, revised by Burton Hobson (Doubleday, 1971), is a comprehensive guide to the world's most popular, most readily available, and most desirable coins.

Coins You Can Collect, by Burton Hobson (Hawthorn, 1970), includes information on numismatic organizations, publications, and the care and handling of your collection.

YEAR-LONG PROJECT   Whenever time permits, the parent and child can draw a map of North and South America (or some part of the world the child chooses), approximately six feet by four feet, to be hung on a wall in the child's room or elsewhere. Throughout the year pictures depicting the climate, products, and industries of particular states or countries are cut from magazines and newspapers and pasted on the map.

SOCIAL STUDIES MAGAZINES   Try to get hold of *National Geographic* magazine, either by subscribing to it yourself or by borrowing it from a friend or the library. This beautiful journal is both pictorial and literary in nature. It spans the globe, opening up the world's nations and cultures to its readers. Other magazines of interest are *Smithsonian*, *Audubon Magazine*, and *Natural History*. (Such magazines contain articles that relate to the science curriculum as well as that of social studies.)

Although the writing in these magazines may be too difficult for your child to read on his own, the illustrations are still beneficial, and the parent can use these magazines as material for reading aloud to the child.

USING THE NEWSPAPER FOR SOCIAL STUDIES   The daily newspaper has been referred to as a living textbook. Worldwide information is conveyed to us on a daily basis, and much of that information can be used by children in activities that reinforce their social studies curriculum. The newspaper can be used with children of all ages.

Topic Picturebooks

Have your child choose a topic from his social studies curriculum that interests him and cut out pictures and articles from the newspaper to paste in his picturebook.

EXAMPLES: *For younger children*

community helpers—pictures of policemen, firemen, politicians, teachers

types of housing and buildings—pictures of apartment buildings, homes, factories, skyscrapers

ways of travel—pictures of cars, trucks, trains

EXAMPLES: *For older children*

Congress at work—pictures of buildings in Washington, D.C.; pictures of the president, senators, congressmen; stories about new laws and legislation

man in space—pictures of astronauts, missiles, and articles on space travel

people of the world—pictures and articles about different countries throughout the world

Using the Newspaper with Maps

Have your child trace a map of the world from an atlas, choose a person in the news such as the secretary of state, and route his travels on the map.

Make a products map of a region or country. Cut pictures from the newspaper showing the products of a particular region or country and paste them on the map.

Local, National, and International News

Have your child locate three stories for news events in each of the following categories: international, national, state, local. He can read the news stories, summarize them, and give his own "news broadcast" to the entire family.

"Who Am I?"
Have your child cut out pictures of people currently in the news, paste them on cardboard, write their names on the back of the card, and play the "Who Am I?" game. One person holds up the picture of the individual, and the other must state who the individual is.

Headline and Picture Collage
With headlines and pictures cut out from newspapers have your child make a collage of current events based on a single theme. He can paste them onto cardboard and then paint them with clear varnish to preserve them.

Cartoons in the News
Political cartoons have been used for centuries for the expression of ideas and opinions in amusing ways. Have your child make a scrapbook of cartoons that explain current events. Discuss with him the meanings conveyed in the illustrations. Have him make up his own cartoons from a news story he has read and formed an opinion on.

"Be a Journalist"
Have your child make his own newspaper with neighborhood friends. They can interview community "celebrities" and local officials and poll the neighborhood with questions concerning current events. Then they can type their information up in news style, have someone with the use of a photocopy machine make copies for them, and sell the copies to the people in the neighborhood.

CURRENT EVENTS   For Election Day, have your child find out the various rules and regulations governing the voting procedure. Make up a list of questions such as Who can vote? How old must one be to vote? Who is running for election? What are their platforms? How many people usually vote during the election? In addition to these questions let the child research the history of voting in the United States and find out, for instance, which people had the vote in 1776, before and after the Civil War, after World War I, after World War II.

For a holiday, have the child research the history of the holiday, how it originated, how it was celebrated in the past, and how this has evolved into its present form.

Take your child to the town meeting, the political rally, or the local political organization headquarters and discuss the reasons why these activities are taking place.

For a short trip or vacation, have your child make a journal or log containing relevant information concerning the area or place to be visited. For example, if the entire family is going to Florida for a vacation, have the child find out the following information from resource books in the library:

Geographic features—location in relation to other land and water areas, type of geographic terrain, climate, and natural resources.

People—how do they work? how is their life-style affected by their environment? what is the population and ethnic composition?

Historical and political background—when did it become a state? who were the first explorers? what famous people came from there? what significant historical events have taken place there? how do the people usually vote?

Agriculture—what crops are grown? what animals are raised?

Industry—what industries are there? what goods are produced? how are the people employed?

Culture and sports—what sports are played and what cultural centers and historic sites should a visitor see?

Resource books and materials available to children in the library or at home are

Encyclopedias.   Through the use of this reference the child gains an understanding of classification, and his concepts are deepened. A reliable source of factual information, it provides background material for teachers and children. It is an important aid in developing the basic reference skills and in establishing habits of consulting authoritative sources and of verifying factual information. Today, encyclopedias are written especially for school-age children. In these encyclopedias the information is presented in language children can understand, and subjects are treated not as isolated entities but in ways that show interrelationships. Among the most widely used encyclopedias in the children's library are: *Compton's Pictured Encyclopedia, Encyclopedia Britannica Junior, The Book of Knowledge,* and *The World Book.*

Almanacs.   These are good sources for current statistical information and detailed coverage of specific facts. Help your child learn how to use the table of contents and index so as to take advantage of the enormous quantity of tightly condensed information contained in these publications. *The World Almanac* and *Information Please Almanac* are widely used.

Atlases.   An atlas contains a collection of maps plus a gazetteer, which contains additional geographic data. To use an atlas properly, children must understand the use of scales, the meaning of map symbols, and how to interpret tables. *The Hammond Contemporary World Atlas* and *Goode's School Atlas* can be found in the children's section of the public library.

Maps and Globes.   Maps and globes are available today in a wide variety, from simple geographical outlines of land and water to highly detailed ones. Three-dimensional maps and globes (usually not in library collections) are lightweight and can be easily handled by young children. Many of these are made of strong plastic and can be marked with paint, crayons, or chalk and then erased with water. The raised relief features of these maps permit the child to "feel" the earth's surfaces. Relief-type maps also provide a three-dimensional effect. Globes are available in a variety of sizes and materials. There are large, lightweight inflatable plastic globes, which can be deflated for easy storage; pictorial relief globes, which give one a realistic three-dimensional view of the earth, and also markable, cleanable globes that can be inexpensively purchased.

Maps and globes can be purchased from a number of companies. Catalogues can be received from the following companies upon request:

George F. Cram Co., Inc., 730 East Washington Street, Indianapolis, Indiana, 46206

Denoyer-Geppert Co., 5235 Ravenswood Avenue, Chicago, Illinois, 60640

C. S. Hammond and Co., Inc., Maplewood, New Jersey 07040

Rand McNally and Co., P.O. Box 7800, Chicago, Illinois 60639

They are also available at department stores, large book stores, and school supply stores.

The First Book of Facts and How to Find Them, by David Whitney, with illustrations by Edward Mackenzie (Watts, 1966), is a guide for the fifth- and sixth-grade child on the use of reference books, tables, maps, and encyclopedias.

Traveling with Children in the U.S.A., A Family Guide to Pleasure, Adventure, Discovery, by Leila Hadley (Americans Discover America Series, 1976), is a guidebook devoted to traveling with children in America that covers each and every state. It is full of thousands of suggestions for year-round family fun.

THE HISTORY OF THE TOWN OR CITY WHERE YOU LIVE   Obtain books from the library on the history of your city or town. If there are no books available, visit city hall or the chamber of commerce and ask for documents concerning the history of the city. The local or state historical society should be helpful.

Obtain maps of the immediate and surrounding areas that show geographical representations of the land.

Study the weather and its effects on the goods that are produced and the way the people live and work.

Find out answers to the following questions:

What famous people lived and visited here? Who were the first inhabitants?

What is the population? Is it increasing or decreasing? Why?

What nationalities make up the population?

What are the major and minor industries?

What areas are densely populated?

Who are the elected officials?

What major contributions has the city or town made to the country?

What major catastrophes have taken place?

7

Science

The Science Curriculum

The elementary school science curriculum is usually composed of a number of areas: living things, Earth in space, magnetism and electricity, sound and light in communication, weather, motion and force in transportation, the earth and its resources, and matter and energy. From prekindergarten through sixth grade these themes are gradually developed from the elementary to the more complex.

Because the science areas, like the language arts areas, so overlap each other throughout the grades and because most activities can be used for a number of grade levels, the parent-child science activities in this book have been divided into two sections. The first is for very young children in prekindergarten, kindergarten, and first grade. These easy activities are meant to give the child science experiences that can be done in the home and the neighborhood and are structured to give the child a very elementary introduction into the world of science. The second section contains a number of activities for children in grades 2 through 6. These activities are designed as a guide for parents to use in planning science activities; they will convert everyday situations in the home and neighborhood into a "science laboratory."

Prekindergarten, Kindergarten, and First Grade

Through observation of the movements and eating habits of classroom animals, children learn the various ways that these animals grow and protect themselves. Through picture books and cards they learn to classify animals and fish according to the environment in which they live—land, water, or air.

By planting seeds, caring for them, and watching them grow they learn that most plants need soil, sun, water, and air to survive. Various fruit pits and vegetable seeds are also planted, and children experience a basic introduction into the way the life cycle perpetuates itself.

Weather as it relates to the kinds of clothing we wear during the different seasons is introduced. The children observe and discuss the different types of weather and often take walks in the neighborhood and park to observe the seasonal changes.

Motion is experienced through play with balls, bicycles and wagons, running and tag games, and through verbal and pictorial classification of the things in the world that move in different ways.

Through their play activities with sand, water, blocks, paints, magnets, and through cooking various foods in the classroom, the children begin to understand, through their senses, the way things work in the world.

SENSORY GAMES   Through the use of their senses children find out about the world. Seeing, hearing, smelling, tasting, and touching are ways of experimenting with things.

The Sense of Smell

You can stimulate an awareness of differences and similarities in the sense of smell by collecting items from the house and neighborhood and keeping them in small jars or plastic bags. Items such as pine needles, leaves, grass, dirt, pebbles, and bark can be collected on a nature walk through the woods or a park. Perfume, vinegar, jelly, pepper, spices, water, dried bread, cloth, paper, and sugar can be collected in the home. You can label the jars with the names of their contents, but encourage your child to recognize the item from the smell only. Ask him questions such as

Which items smell pleasant?

What smells sweet? What smells sour?

Which items do not have a smell?

Which items have a very strong smell?

Have him classify the items in groups according to how they smell.

When your child is familiar with the scents of these objects, play a guessing game—"What Is It?" Blindfold him and have him guess what he is smelling.

Sniff Poems, illustrated by Lisl Weil (Scholastic Book Services, 1975), is a truly remarkable book containing poems by famous poets, each poem with a different scent to match its theme. The child must scratch a patch of paper, which then releases the scent of strawberry, orange, gingerbread, chocolate, and many more.

The Sense of Taste

Talk about the different tastes of the foods we eat. Do pickles taste like potato chips? Why not? What do potato chips have that pickles do not? How do potato chips taste after they are dunked in a glass of water? How does a cookie taste before and after it has been dunked in a glass of milk? Taste a lemon, a piece of candy, a sardine, and a pickle. Which tastes bitter, sweet, salty, sour? Have your child hold his nose and taste these things again. How do they taste now?

Once again, blindfold your child and see if he can identify these things by taste alone.

As your child eats his food, talk about the texture of the different foods.

Which foods are hard and crunchy?

Which foods are soft and creamy?

Which foods are chewy?

Which foods do we eat hot, and which cold?

How do carrots taste before we cook them and how do they taste after we cook them?

The Sense of Hearing

Collect items that make different sounds: cardboard, nails, paper, plastic, wood, nylon, cloth.

What sounds do these objects make when they are dropped onto the floor or rubbed together?

Which sounds are pleasant, which are harsh?

Can you identify the sound I make without looking?

Listen to the sounds in the street, in the park, and in the zoo as you stroll through the neighborhood with your child.

Play the "Animal Sounds" game with your child: The parent imitates the sound of a dog, cat, lion, horse, donkey, duck, pig, bird, as well as other animals, and your child must guess the animal.

The Sense of Touch

Collect items that are rough, smooth, light, heavy, flexible, or straight and place them in a paper bag. Have your child guess what the items are without looking.

Play the game called "Find Me Something That Is . . ." by asking him to find something in the room that is soft, hard, smooth, rough, wet, warm, cold.

The Sense of Sight

Leaf through magazines looking for different colors. Categorize pictures of things in magazines in terms of their different shapes, sizes, textures, positions, and weather conditions.

Look for shapes in traffic signs, window frames, apartment buildings, ice-cream cones, and wheels.

Keep a magnifying glass handy so that your child can take a closer look at the things of our world. Have him inspect things in the house as well as outside, such as insects, plants, grass, twigs, and leaves.

MAGNET FUN

"What Things Do Magnets Pull?"

Collect various items in a box, such as leaves, nails, rubber bands, screws, bolts, pins, marbles, twigs, paper clips, and paper. Explain to your child that articles that have iron in them can be pulled by a magnet. Have him divide the objects into two piles. Ask him: "What other things can you find in the house that can be pulled by a magnet?"

"Magnet Fishing Game"

Attach a magnet to the end of a three-foot-long string and the other end of the string to a stick. Cut out ten fish shapes from cardboard and have the child color them. Attach a large paper clip to the mouth of each fish and place them in a box. The child must "catch" the fish with his magnetic fishing pole.

"Magnetic Puppet Show"

Cut out pictures of people and objects from magazines and paste them onto cardboard or heavy paper. Cut the cardboard into the same shape as the picture. Tape a paper clip to the back of each picture. Use heavy paper as a base. By moving a magnet behind the base paper, the objects will move. The figures and objects can act out the child's story.

WATER AND SAND PLAY   Young children are fascinated by water and sand. For experience in water play, use the kitchen sink, bathtub, or a water basin. Provide some pans and water holders for your child to use. Funnels, plastic or rubber tubing, pump squirts and straws are also helpful, in addition to things that float (cork, wood, plastic) and things that sink (lead, coins, pebbles).

Through such play children learn how water takes the shape of its container, how some things float and other things sink, and vocabulary such as *full-empty, hot-cold, float-sink, half-full/half-empty*.

A wooden or strong cardboard box filled with a few buckets of sand from the beach or lumberyard will give your child the same type of learning experiences as water play.

Pouring water and sand is also a good exercise for developing eye-hand coordination.

At this age children are able to participate in household chores in a limited but helpful fashion. After their play time with sand and water they should help with cleaning up. Small brooms and dust pans are available for children; they can use these to sweep up the sand, and sponges can be used for cleaning up any excess water. These are learning experiences too.

WEATHER   Talk about the weather as you are helping your child dress to go outside so he becomes aware of how we dress in relation to the weather conditions.

When you are walking or driving with your child, discuss the seasonal changes. Collect leaves, twigs, pine cones, and berries that are of a seasonal nature.

Keep a thermometer in the kitchen window and have your child look at the temperature reading every day.

Watch the weather report on television together.

Divide a paper plate into four pie sections with crayon and a ruler.

Label the four sections *sunny day*, *partly cloudy*, *overcast*, and *rain*, and draw a picture that goes along with each caption. Attach a cardboard arrow to the center of the plate with a paper fastener. Hang it on the refrigerator door or in your child's room. Have your child observe the weather conditions when he gets up in the morning and point the arrow on the plate to the type of day it is, or else use the evening forecast to tell you what kind of day it will be.

From magazines and calendars collect pictures of a sunny day, a cloudy day, a rainy day, a spring day, and a fall day, a summer day at the beach, and a winter day in the mountains. Have your child talk about the pictures and make a "Season Weather Book" with them by pasting them onto construction paper and stapling the pages together.

OBSERVING ANIMALS   Neighborhood walks to the park enable children to observe the animals. Bring some bread and nuts to feed the fish, birds, and squirrels.

Visit the zoo, the aquarium, the museum of natural history and, if possible, a nearby farm.

A bird feeder placed outside a window or in the backyard will allow your child to get a closer look at the habits of birds.

Picture books from the library allow children to study other animals as well. In discussing these pictures with your child, point out the animals that fly, walk, swim, hop, and crawl.

Compare a dog, a cat, a fish, a bird, and a worm.

> What covers their bodies?
>
> How do they move?
>
> What foods do they eat?
>
> What color, size, and shape are they?
>
> Where do they live?
>
> When do we see them?

There are many field guides available that parents can use with their children. Although such guides are published for older children and adults, parents can use them with very young children by pointing out and discussing pictures of the animals and birds that inhabit our world. Some of them are

Complete Field Guide to American Wildlife by Henry Collins (Harper and Row, 1959).

A Field Guide to the Mammals by William Burt and Richard Grossenheider (Houghton Mifflin, 1964).

A Field Guide to the Birds by Roger Tory Peterson (Houghton Mifflin, 1947).

Wild Animals of North America by the National Geographic Society (National Geographic, 1960).

WATCHING YOURSELF GROW   Have your child trace an outline of his hand and foot every two or three months. Paste the drawings into a notebook with the date. As the months go by, he will see the steady growth of his hand and foot.

With a tape, measure parts of your child's body, such as his head, waist, arms, and legs, every few months. Record the changes for him in his "Growing Up Book." Include in the book any pictures you have taken of him.

Pick a place in the house such as the inside of a closet door to measure the height of your child and mark it with the date. Over the months and years he will be able to "see" the change. Record his growth in both English and metric measurements.

COOKING TASTEFULLY   Have your child help you prepare meals. If you are baking, let him knead the dough; let him toss the salad, make the hamburger patties, or pour and stir the ingredients for a cake. Talk about the change in the substances when they are mixed together and when they are cooked.

Have him make play dough. You need 1½ cups of flour, ½ cup of salt, ½ cup of water, and ¼ cup of vegetable oil or liquid detergent. Mix the flour and salt and slowly add the water and oil. Knead the dough well and add some food coloring. (You can preserve the play dough by keeping it in a plastic bag in the refrigerator.)

COLLECTIONS   Children love to collect things. Such collections can be useful science experiences. Collecting rocks, shells, and leaves enables the young child to become more aware of the things that are happening around them. A magnifying glass will help your child observe the characteristics of such objects more carefully.

A rock collection is an especially easy collection for children of this age. Besides the obvious elementary science education that takes place, children also gain reinforcement in the other subject areas:

language arts —in terms of classification of colors, size, shape
math—in terms of weight, measurement, counting
social studies —in terms of where rocks were found, how they were
   formed, how man uses rocks (marble, slate, etc.)

Many different rocks can be found on walks through the neighborhood and in the park. Label them with your child and discuss how they feel, how they are alike or different, their color, shape, and size. As you walk through the neighborhood with your child, point out buildings, sidewalks, streets, and walls that are made from different types of rock materials.

At the beach he can collect shells and driftwood. With crayons and paint he can decorate the shells, and with the parent's help he can varnish the driftwood and make lovely household decorations.

Leaves can be collected on a nature walk through the park. To preserve them, arrange two or three fresh leaves between two sheets of waxed paper. Place sheets of newspaper above and below the waxed paper and gently iron over the layers several times. Tape or paste the picture onto another piece of paper and write the name of the leaf, what tree the leaf is from, and where you found the leaf.

(For books on all kinds of collections, see pages 167-168).

"WHERE IS MY SHADOW?"   Ask the child where his shadow is. Tell him to go behind a tree and see if it is still there. Ask him to think about when we can see our shadow and when we can't. Have him look for long shadows of buildings, trees, and telephone poles. Make scary shadows with a flashlight in the dark. Use your hands and a flashlight to tell a shadow story and have him do the same.

Make a sundial in the backyard by putting a stick into the ground so that it is standing up straight. Have him look at it in the morning and see where the shadow is. Find out where the shadow is at noon, at five o'clock in the afternoon.

Have your child stand on a cement sidewalk at nine o'clock in the morning while you draw his shadow on the ground with chalk. Do this at different times as the day goes on. Explain to him how the sun's rays come from different directions and cause the shadows to fall differently.

Use a globe and a flashlight to show him how night is the result of the rotation of the earth.

Play shadow tag. Instead of tagging the other person, the individual who is "it" must step on the shadows of the players.

Read the story *My Shadow and I*, by Patty Wolcott, illustrated by Frank Bozzo (Addison-Wesley, 1975), about how a young boy and his shadow conquer a monster.

PLANTS   There are some plants that we look at and smell and others that we eat.

Leaf through magazines with your child and have him point out the plants that we eat, such as celery, tomatoes, apples, lettuce, oranges, pears, cabbage, and so on. Have him cut out these pictures and paste them into a scrapbook on plants.

Draw pictures of roses, daisies, violets, tulips as examples of plants that normally we do not eat and have your child color them.

Take a trip to the botanical gardens or a commercial nursery to admire the different plants and flowers that beautify our world. On another family outing visit a farm and look for any plants that we eat.

What do plants need to grow? Take four weed plants of the same approximate size from your backyard or a nearby woods. Place one in soil in a plastic container. Keep it in the sun and water it daily. Pull the second weed out of its soil and lay it on a sheet of paper. Put the third weed in a container with soil and leave it in the sun, but do not water it. Put the fourth weed in a bag so no sunlight can get at it. Have your child draw pictures of what happens to the four plants. Discuss with him the things that plants need to grow.

Plants grow toward the sun. Place a plant in a window where it gets light only from the one side. Observe each day how the plant has turned more toward the light.

To show your child how water gets up to the leaves of plants, put a fresh stalk of celery in a beaker of water that is colored with red ink or food coloring. Your child will be able to observe how the ink moves up the tubes of the stem into the leaves.

Make a "Mini Garden": Grow a grass lawn on a sponge by sprinkling some seed on it and setting it in water. Your child can mow his lawn with a pair of scissors. Or fill each space of an egg carton with soil and plant some seeds in the soil. Place the container in the sun and sprinkle it with water every day.

MACHINES   Have your child look through magazines for pictures of machines, cut them out, and paste them in a booklet entitled "My Machine Book."

Look around. How many machines can he find in the house? Ask him what machines we see in the street and what machines are up in the air.

Play "Name That Machine": The parent makes the sound of different machines, such as a car engine, an airplane, a bell, a horn, a drill, a locomotive, and the child must guess what machine it is.

Second Through Sixth Grades

Children on these grade levels are capable of taking part in in-depth science experiences. Such activities can provide the entire family with exciting field trips in the outdoors as well as indoor activities for rainy days.

Science is everywhere. A walk in the fields, taking care of plants and animals, observing and recording the weather changes, cooking, and even the birth of a new family member can serve as reinforcing science experiences for the elementary school child.

Like every other subject area, science involves the memorization of facts and the understanding of concepts. The real excitement of science, however, involves hands-on activities in which children are able to interact with things in our world, thus becoming more involved in their learning experiences. Such activities give richer meaning to the necessarily passive activities of reading, listening, memorizing, and understanding. When a child is given the opportunity to care for and observe the activities of plants and animals, he can actually see in concrete examples the various abstract concepts of evolution, the needs of living creatures and plants, and the similarities and differences between the plant and animal kingdoms and the human species. And in seeing such phenomena, he is able to understand more clearly.

Pets and Insects

Pets provide fun for children and teach them the responsibility of caring for animals. Through such interaction, children learn about animals' needs for food, shelter, and sleep. Dogs, cats, tadpoles, gerbils, hamsters, and guinea pigs are good pets for children. And by catching insects such as butterflies, crickets, ants, and spiders and maintaining a proper living environment for them, children can investigate the mysterious ways of the insect world.

TADPOLES   Tadpoles can be an interesting science experience for children as they watch the tadpole go through its life cycle and turn into a frog. (They do not need daily attention.) Tadpoles can be found in the early spring along the banks of streams, lakes, or ponds. They are most easily caught with a net. They can also be bought in aquarium supply shops. Fill the tank with water brought from the tadpole's original environment. If you must use tap water, let it set for twenty-four hours before placing the tadpoles in the tank, to allow for chemical dissipation. Feed them commercial fish food and scraped beef or liver. Some books that will help your child in his investigation into the life cycle of toads and frogs are

A Frog Is Born by William White (Sterling, 1972)

Toad by Anne and Harlow Rockwell (Doubleday, 1972)

Let's Find Out About Frogs by Corinne Naden (Watts, 1972)

With some careful searching on the banks of a pond, your child may be able to find frog eggs, which are housed in a jellylike substance that floats in the water. The small black dots in the substance are the tadpoles. If he cannot find any eggs, he may be able to purchase them in a local aquarium supply shop. Some questions for your child to consider as he observes his eggs and tadpoles are

What shape and size are the eggs?

Describe the protective covering surrounding the eggs.

Do the tadpoles emerge from their jelly mass together or do they come out separately?

Sketch the appearance of the tadpole as it first emerges from the jelly.

How do they move?

What physical characteristics do you observe in their growth? (Check twice a day.)

How much time passes before limbs begin to appear?

Which appear first, front or rear limbs?

When does the tadpole begin breathing air?

HIBERNATING FROGS   Once your child's tadpoles have turned into frogs, you can do an easy kitchen experiment with them to show how cold-blooded animals lower their temperature to that of the surrounding water or soil. Fill two pans with moist soil and place them in the refrigerator for a day, until the soil becomes very cold. Place two frogs in an aquarium tank with one inch of water on the bottom. Place three pieces of ice in the water every minute until the frogs are packed in ice. When the frogs no longer move, place each one in its own pan of cold soil. Then replace the pans in the refrigerator, leaving them for one or two days. The frogs will be in their hibernating state, in which they do not breathe or eat. The oxygen the frog needs enters its body through its skin. After a day or two in the refrigerator place one pan in the sunlight or another warm place and put the other pan in a cooler place. As the temperature warms the soil, the frogs become warm also and will return to their natural active state just as frogs do in the spring after hibernating for the winter.

GERBILS   Gerbils can be easily housed in a large fish tank or gerbil cage purchased in pet shops or department stores. Wood shavings or commercial litter should cover the bottom of the cage. Put a turning wheel in the cage to give the gerbils some exercise. If you purchase a male and a female gerbil, you will give your child the exciting opportunity of watching them build a nest, give birth, and raise their young.

Have your child keep a record of his observations in his own logbook. Explain to him that scientists keep logbooks so that they can keep a record of their experiments and observations and also to be able to recheck their work for accuracy. Some things he might want to record in his logbook concerning gerbils are

what foods they eat

how much time they spend sleeping, burrowing, and exercising

how many days pass before baby gerbils open their eyes . . . begin leaving the nest . . . eat gerbil food

how similar and how different are male and female gerbil activities

AQUARIUMS   Both fresh and salt water aquariums are easily maintained in the home and can be left for a number of days without care. Visit your local pet shop and ask the manager for a few different types of fish that will reproduce in a home aquarium. Borrow books from the library to help plan for the needs of the fish. Some books your child can borrow from the library follow:

Tropical Saltwater Aquariums, by Seymour Simon, with illustrations by Karl Stuecklen (Viking, 1976), provides the necessary information and advice on aquariums—their equipment and maintenance—and on suitable fish and their care.

Aquariums, by Phillip Steinberg, with pictures by George Overlie (Lerner, 1975), is a book that illustrates the basics of tank preparation and maintenance and discusses the selection and care of tropical fish and other water creatures and plants.

The First Book of Fishes, by Jeanne Bendick (Watts, 1965), describes the various habits and characteristics of many different varieties of fish.

DOGS   Over 40 percent of American families own a dog. A dog can become the center of some of the most pleasurable and positive learning experiences for your child. Helping to care for a dog, feed it, bathe it, groom it, walk it, and even train it can be a wonderful experience. It is a fine way to observe animal behavior, to study creatures different from us yet with things in common. The sense of pride and accomplishment that can come from this activity can spread to everything a child does. A truly beautiful book that can be interesting to both children and parents for working with your dog is *Dog Training for Kids* by Carol Lea Benjamin (Howell Book House, 1976). This do-it-yourself manual written especially for kids in a light, funny, upbeat style contains clear instructions for caring for and training dogs.

ANTS   Ants are fascinating creatures to observe, since, like man, they take care of their young and they feed and help each other. Children can make a simple ant cage with a half-gallon jar, black paper, a piece of wood, a shallow pan of water, and a small piece of sponge. Have your child dig up the soil around an anthill and place it in the jar. To have a thriving ant community a queen ant is needed to lay eggs. The queen can be recognized by its size, which is bigger than that of any other ants. Wrap the black paper around the jar to simulate the darkness that exists underground; this will encourage the ants to dig close enough to the glass for the tunnels to be observed. Place the jar on a piece of wood in the middle of a shallow pan of water to keep the ants from running away. Saturate a small piece of sponge with water and then place it on the top of the soil to keep it moist. Place some sweet food on top of the soil as food for the ants. When your child wants to observe the ants, he should remove the paper from the jar.

Ant farms can also be purchased in most pet and large department stores. Your child might like to read some of the following books about ant life:

Biography of an Ant by Alice Hopf (Putnam's, 1974)

A Closer Look at Ants by Valerie Pitt and David Cook (Watts, 1975)

Ants by Helen Hoke (Watts, 1970)

CATERPILLARS AND COCOONS   Go for a nature walk in the spring and find a caterpillar. Place it with leaves and sticks in a jar and cover the jar with a top that allows air to enter. Sprinkle a little water on the leaves every few days, and if necessary place more leaves in the jar for the caterpillar to eat. The caterpillar will spin a cocoon from which a moth or butterfly will emerge. *Caterpillars and How They Live*, by Robert McClung (Morrow, 1965), and *The Beginning Book of Butterflies*, by Kathy Sammis (Macmillan, 1965), are two informative books for children.

CRICKETS   In Japan and China people keep crickets in cages for pets because of the beauty they find in listening to the cricket's song. A cricket is a little black or brown insect with long hind legs that enable it to jump fast. Children can find crickets during warm summer evenings by walking toward the sound of the cricket, locating it with a flashlight, and then quickly covering it with a jar so it does not get away. If your child cannot catch one, he might be able to purchase some in a fish bait or aquarium store. Damp sand or earth placed in a cardboard box with tiny holes punched in the side to allow air to enter and a plastic covering over the top of the box will provide a good cage. Crickets eat small pieces of apple, melon, whole wheat bread, chicken or meat, and other insects such as flies. Without a balanced diet, crickets may chew their way through the walls of the cage and even eat each other. Male crickets, the ones with the curved lines on their wings, do the singing.

Some good books about animals and insects follow:

Shelf Pets: How To Take Care of Small Wild Animals by Edward Ricciuti, with photographs by Arline Strong (Harper and Row, 1971), is a very good book describing the care of animals such as frogs, lizards, crayfish, water striders, turtles, and salamanders.

You Can Make an Insect Zoo by Hortense Roberta Roberts, with photographs by Francis Munger (Chicago Press, 1974), tells about insects, how to catch and care for them, and of course, how to build an insect zoo.

The Golden Exploring Earth Book Series (Golden Press), is a series of books that introduces beginning scientists and nature lovers to the marvels and wonders of the earth. The beautiful and true-to-life illustrations make these books good for primary as well as intermediate grade children. Some of the recommended titles are *Animals, Insects, Dinosaurs, Nature Hikes, Reptiles and Amphibians*; there are many others. These books are available at children's bookstores for less than a dollar.

The How and Why Wonder Books (Grosset and Dunlap) is another series of books that introduce children to the world of science and nature. Lively illustrations and interesting text enable these books to be recommended for all elementary school children. Some titles are *Primitive Man, Fish, Wild Flowers, Weather, Ecology*; there are many others. These are also available at children's bookstores for less than a dollar.

Growing Plants

A good science experience that also lends itself to making your home more beautiful is growing and caring for plants. From this experience children begin to learn about the needs of plants, how people use plants, and the names, colors, and shapes of the plants in our world.

TERRARIUMS Terrariums are man-made homes for plants. To make a terrarium, your child will need plants of different sizes, some rich soil, charcoal, pebbles or stones, and an aquarium tank or large jar. A trip to the park or a nearby field will enable your child to gather some plants, moss, twigs, and bark. Place a thin layer of pebbles in the bottom of the tank and then put pieces of charcoal over the pebbles (the charcoal will absorb gases and help to keep the soil from becoming sour). Then place an inch or two of soil over the charcoal and wet it a little. Transplant the plants into the soil and cover the rest of the soil with the moss, twigs, and bark. Brightly colored stones will help to beautify the terrarium. Place a small dish in the soil to hold water and then cover the tank with a sheet of glass or transparent paper.

Have your child observe the changes that take place in the terrarium. The water will evaporate and condense as the temperature changes so that it will seem to rain in the terrarium. If the terrarium is too dry, some plants will wither, and if it is too wet, mold may appear.

Your child can make different sized terrariums using different sized jars. Other variations will depend on the kind of plants you use and your imagination in creating scenic backgrounds with colored pebbles and rocks.

Terrariums, by John Hoke (Watts, 1972), discusses the necessary materials for making a terrarium and provides suggestions on plants, soils, and enclosures that create a healthy environment.

HERBARIUMS   A herbarium is a collection of pressed plants kept for scientific purposes. Each plant is mounted on a separate sheet of paper, on which is written the name of the plant, and where and when it was located. In order to press plants for preservation purposes, they must be dried quickly and thoroughly. All the juices must be pressed from the plant. This can be done by placing the flattened plant between two pieces of blotting paper, which are then placed between two boards. Pressure is applied to the boards by placing them in a vise or by placing very heavy objects on them. After a day or so remove the boards and check to see if the plant is completely dry. If it is not, do the same thing over again with new blotting paper. When the plant is completely dry, use rubber cement to paste it onto pieces of stiff paper. The child can label the different parts of the plant and keep his herbarium collection in a loose-leaf binder. Here are some books your child can use to identify the various plants:

Plants Grow, by Thomas Tinsley (Putnam's, 1971), for second- and third-graders, depicts plant development with line drawings and a simple text.

Plants, by Leslie Waller (Grosset and Dunlap, 1967), provides a child's introduction to the plant world.

The Pictorial Encyclopedia of Plants and Flowers, by F. A. Novak (Crown, 1966), provides photographs and information on every aspect of plant life, from one-celled algae to complex trees.

WINDOWSILL PLANTS   Windowsill plants can include tomatoes, peppers, zinnias, and marigolds, as well as geraniums, coleus, ferns, ivy, begonias, and bulbs of different kinds. Waxed paper cups or pint-sized milk containers are convenient for growing seeds. Packages of seeds can be purchased at the supermarket or your local plant store. Plant the seeds in separate containers in a few inches of soil and sprinkle them with water. Most seeds grow faster when they are kept in a dark place until they begin to sprout, at which point they should be moved to a place where they can get plenty of sunlight. Add some plant food or fertilizer from time to time once the seeds have begun to grow. As they get larger they can be transplanted to larger pots and even outdoors.

Orange, lemon, grapefruit, and tangerine seeds can also grow into lovely household plants. Immediately after removing the seeds from the fruit soak them in water for about twenty-four hours. Then plant them in a handful of sand mixed with potting soil about one-half inch deep. Keep the plants moist on a daily basis and water them about twice a week. While the seeds are germinating, you might want to cover them with plastic wrap or a plastic tray in order to create a greenhouse effect for good growth.

Avocado Plants

An avocado pit placed in a jar with only the tip submerged in water will grow roots. Toothpicks can be used to support the pit. Germination usually takes about thirty days. When the roots, stem, and a few leaves appear, it should be planted in soil, so that the top half of the pit is above the soil level. Good potting soil mixed with a little sand and some peat should be used. Keep it in the sun and water it whenever it looks dry. Home-grown avocado plants, with the proper care, can grow to five feet. Don't forget to transplant it as it gets bigger and bigger.

Pineapple Plants

Cut off the leafy top and about one inch of the pineapple. Use soil mixed with some gravel or sand and plant the pineapple up to the bottom of the crown. The back of pineapple leaves have small cups. Pour water into these cups and keep them full of water.

Pea Plants

Fill a drinking glass three quarters full with cotton wool. Add water until the cotton is soaking wet. Take two or three fresh green peas and place them between the side of the glass and the cotton. Place the peas in a dark place until they sprout roots. Then put the glass in a sunny window. When the plants have grown to about two or three inches, transplant them into a container of earth. Keep the soil moist and pods will grow on the plant.

Tomato Plants

Fill a cake pan or tin foil container with moist potting soil. Make two or three rows in the soil each about one half inch deep. Lay your tomato seeds each about one half inch apart in the rows but do not cover them with soil. Take a sheet of newspaper and place it on top of the container. Sprinkle the seeds with water whenever the soil looks dry. When tiny seed leaves appear, place the container in a sunny window and keep the soil moist for a day or two. When the leaves seem strong enough, transplant each seedling into a larger container. Keep the containers in the sun and make sure the soil is moist.

If you start growing your tomato seeds in the middle of April, you should have tomatoes for your salad by midsummer.

Potato Plants

You can grow your own potatoes in just a few months at any time of the year. Take a large pot, place some stones on the bottom, and then fill it with potting soil. Take a potato and plant it about six inches from the surface. In only a few days sprouts will appear. Keep the plant in a place where there is a lot of light. When the plant has grown to about a foot high, blossoms will appear. Then the leaves will begin to turn yellow and fall. At this time dig up the plant. If you are lucky or have a green thumb, you should have a yield of two or three potatoes.

Growing a Green Thumb by Lorraine Surcouf (Barons Educational Series, 1975), is a terrific book for the young gardener. Parents can use this book with children for all types of plants, from narcissi to tomatoes.

Kids Gardening: A First Indoor Gardening Book, by Aileen Paul, with illustrations by Arthur Hawkins (Doubleday, 1972), contains easy-to-follow instructions on basic materials and methods for growing plants.

Indoor Gardening Fun, by Milton Carlton, with illustrations by Novie Ahrenhold (Reilly and Lee, 1970), contains instructions for growing a variety of plants indoors from seeds, bulbs, roots, and cuttings.

Reproduction

Many schools have an entire curriculum dealing with reproduction. Such programs begin in the first and second grades with informal discussions that arise out of children's questions concerning classroom observations such as the birth of gerbils or guppies. By the fourth grade, reproduction is being fully discussed as a subject in the grade's curriculum. It concerns the study of life cycles in plant, animal, and human development. Such studies include the reproduction process, birth, and the growth to maturity of the various species. How conception comes about, the length of the gestation period, and the necessary preparation for young are explained. Included in the study of the birth process are the time period of infancy, dependency on parents, and the various growth stages. From these topics the children receive a solid structure of knowledge concerning the basic facts of reproduction, sexuality, and family structure.

Even if the school does not provide for such experiences, sooner or later, as every parent knows, the child will ask, "Where do babies come from?" The question must be answered, for if it is evaded, the child will ask the same question of one of his friends and will probably receive an answer that is only partly correct. Children's questions are the proof of their learning and the stepping stones of knowledge. Parents should deal with such questions from their own experience and common sense. Some helpful guidelines might be

> Keep in mind the general maturity level of your child.
>
> Keep the discussion informal and comfortable.
>
> Keep your answers brief and to the point without undue explanation of more than what the child is really curious about. If he is unhappy with your explanation, he will ask you further questions.

Don't be afraid to use the proper vocabulary concerning sexual organs and physical relationships. Words such as *penis*, *vagina*, and *intercourse* may have certain personal connotations to adults because of our own upbringing, but to children they are just new words.

Be attentive to evasive questions. Many children who are going through puberty are shy and may be even a little fearful about asking questions concerning such matters, even though they are desirous of learning the answers. Because of their shyness or fear they may ask an evasive question such as "Is it bad to think about things or have dreams about certain things?" If your child asks such a question, try to lead him into a discussion that will make him comfortable in asking the questions he might have.

Besides these informal discussions, children can involve themselves in many projects that will enable them to learn about the facts of sexual reproduction as well as reinforce the rest of their science curriculum. Some of them are

ANIMAL REPRODUCTION   Many animals are born and develop without the care of their parents. Purchase some fish, frog, snail, and turtle eggs from your local pet shop and have your child observe and record the life cycles of these independent creatures.

Fur-bearing animals give birth to their babies and care for them by feeding them and providing shelter and safety for them. Gerbils, mice, cats, and dogs will afford your child the exciting opportunity to watch how these animals prepare for and give birth to their offspring and how they care for them after birth. (See pages 155-159 for care of animals.)

Some good books that children can read concerning animal reproduction follow:

The Life Cycle of Butterflies, by Ronald Ridout and Michael Holt, with illustrations by Tony Payne (Grosset and Dunlap, 1974), identifies the common species of butterflies and explains courtship patterns, mating, and basic life processes during each stage of the butterfly's growth and development.

The Life Cycle of Cats, by the same authors (Grosset and Dunlap, 1974), considers such topics as evolution, mating, reproduction, and cat care.

An Earthworm Is Born, by William White, Jr. (Sterling, 1975), follows the earthworm through its life cycle, describing its anatomy and ecological importance.

The First Days of Life, by Russell Freedman, with drawings by Joseph Cellini (Holiday, 1974), describes the experiences of codfish, turtle, herring gull, robin, wolf, elephant, dolphin and chimpanzee young immediately after birth.

HUMAN REPRODUCTION   The beginning of a new life, the birth of a human being, is only another step in the life cycle of that individual that began nine months before out of an act of intercourse between a man and a woman. Children want to know why and how, and it is often not easy for parents to explain such things to their children. The following activities will help parents be more comfortable in their role of advisor to their children concerning sexual matters as well as adding to the child's learning in science.

Photographs

Collect photographs of your family starting with your child and going as far back as possible, including parents, uncles, aunts, cousins, grandparents, and great-grandparents on both sides of the family. Arrange them in genealogical order in an album so that your child can see his place in the family evolution.

Television

Watch for television specials on birth, the family structure, the various developmental stages of human growth, and the life cycles of animals, insects, and plants. Discuss the program with your child as well as the differences in the life cycles of humans and animals.

Reproduction Book

Have your child choose a plant, an animal, an insect, and a fish, borrow books from the library concerning their life cycles. Then have him make a book of his own, writing down summaries of how these living creatures reproduce and live. Have him include his own drawings of the process for each life cycle, including information concerning method of reproduction, gestation period, preparation for young, birth and infancy, dependency, growth stages, maturity.

Library Books
Here are some good books parents can purchase or borrow from the library on human reproduction:

The Reproduction System: How Living Things Multiply, by Alvin Silverstein and Virginia Silverstein, with illustrations by Lee Ames (Prentice-Hall, 1971), compares the human reproductive system with that of other organisms.

Twins, by Joanna Cole and Madeline Edmondson, with drawings by Salvatore Raciti (Morrow, 1972), describes the stages in the pre-natal growth of identical and fraternal twins and discusses the role of heredity in their development.

Twenty-Eight Days, by Kathleen Elgin and John Osterritter (McKay, 1973), describes the meaning of and myths about menstruation and explains the menstrual cycle.

Man and Woman, by Julian May (Follett, 1969), discusses the emotional and physical changes that take place in puberty, adult sexuality, and the physical and emotional relationship of marriage.

How Was I Born? A Story in Pictures, by Lennart Nilsson (Delacorte/Seymour Lawrence, 1975), presents photographs, illustrations, and a scientifically accurate text to teach children about conception, fetal development, birth, and sex.

Nature Walks

A family outing that can combine fun and learning is a nature hike. Such walks can take place in fields, through woods, along streams, around lakes or marshes or along the seashore. Each of these environments contains a multitude of exciting aspects of nature to be discovered by those with a discerning eye, a soft step, and a few guidebooks. Some careful preparation will allow your child to get the most benefit from his adventure. Some helpful guidelines follow:

Decide on the type of environment you will explore and borrow books from the library that contain information about the animals, birds, plants, insects, and trees that exist in the area you will visit. Some basic field guides that can be helpful are

A Field Guide to the Birds by Roger Tory Peterson (Houghton Mifflin, 1947)

Golden Nature Guides: Insects, Birds, Mammals, Seashores, Reptiles and Amphibians, Fishes, Butterflies and Moths, Zoology by Herbert Zim and others (Simon and Schuster, 1949–1968)

Common Insects of North America by Lester Swann and Charles Papp (Harper and Row, 1972)

American Wild Flowers by Harold Moldenke (Van Nostrand Reinhold, 1950)

Trees by George Sullivan (Follett, 1970)

A magnifying glass and a pair of field glasses, a few jars for collecting insects, a net for catching butterflies and moths, a few plastic bags for collecting leaves, soil, rocks, or shells are good items to bring along with you. Also, don't forget a trowel or small shovel for digging, as well as a pair of gloves.

Dress comfortably, wear a good pair of walking shoes, and bring along a comfortable sitting pillow.

If possible, arrive at your destination before sunrise to afford yourself the opportunity of watching and listening as nature awakens.

Things to do on your walk:

1. Turn over rocks and logs to examine insect environments. When you do this, be careful that you don't disturb any animals that might bite. Use a magnifying glass to observe the living things. Take samples of rotting logs, soil, ferns, leaves, shells, feathers, and berries to be examined at home. *Outdoor Things to Do*, by William Hillcourt (Golden Press, 1975); *The Doubleday Nature Encyclopedia*, by Angela Sheehan (Doubleday, 1973); and *The Complete Family Nature Guide*, by Jean Worthley (Doubleday, 1976) all offer suggestions for observing nature.

2. Collect samples of living animals and insects, such as tadpoles, ants, worms, minnows, grasshoppers, caterpillars. Have your child use these creatures to start his own insect zoo. (See pages 155-159).

3. Collect items for rock, shell, leaf, and plant collections. Some books that will help your child with his collection are listed here:

The Rock Hound's Book, by Seymour Simon (Viking, 1976), for children in the fifth and sixth grade, provides a guide to finding and identifying rocks and minerals for starting collections.

Collecting Small Fossils, by Lois Hussey and Catherine Pessino (Crowell, 1970), for third- and fourth-graders, shows children how they can collect small fossils.

Natural History Collecting, by Reg Harris (Grosset and Dunlap, 1972), for fifth- and sixth-graders includes the various techniques involved in collecting specimens of North American rocks, plants, and animals.

Collecting Seashells, by Kathleen Johnstone (Grosset and Dunlap, 1970), is actually for older children, but it can be used by parents and children together. It is a guide for collecting, storing, and cataloguing shell specimens.

The Junior Book of Insects, by Edwin Teale (Dutton, 1972), for fifth- and sixth-graders, is a guide to the collection and observation of common insects.

(See pages 155-159 for other books on collections.)

NOTE: These books can be used by children of all ages as long as the parent provides some help in reading them with their children.

4. Over a period of a year have your child investigate the changes that take place in the environment during the four seasons. He can do this by picking four neighborhood things: a tree, a grassy field, a nearby pond, lake, or stream, and a plant such as a rosebush or some other common local flower. Here are some activities that he can do in the middle of each season:

Make a chart and briefly describe the seasonal conditions and changes. An example of such a chart might be

SEASONAL CHART
Observations of: *An Oak Tree*

Date: July 24, 19—
Season: Summer
Time: 12:30 P.M.
Weather: Sunny and clear 85 degrees F
Leaves: green and full
Animal activity: five birds in tree, one squirrel, ants on ground
Colors of tree: bark—brown, leaves—green

Soil around tree: soft, warm, and moist
Circumference of tree: twenty-three inches
Length of observation: 1 hour

Have your child take photographs of the thing he is observing.

Collect samples of the environment (pond water, soil, leaves, flow-ers, grass) during each season and record the changes that can be seen in the samples. The child can do experiments with these samples such as

1. Dig up a bucket of soil in the early winter, before the ground has frozen, and examine it, then cover it and place it in a warm spot in the house for several days; then observe the changes that have taken place.

2. Take some pond water and observe it with a magnifying glass. After the child records his observations, he should heat some of the water, boil some of it, freeze some of it, and add tap water to some of it, observing and recording the changes that take place in the various samples.

3. Use leaves and plants to make herbariums and terrariums. (See pages 159-163 for instructions.)

Cooking

Cooking is not only an enjoyable and creative experience, it can be a science experience also. By observing your child you will be able to see what skills of cooking he is ready to master—stirring, peeling, grating, scrambling, shelling, slicing, dicing, paring, washing, melting, and so on.

Some parents make the mistake of having children only do the chore aspects of cooking—setting the table, cleaning up, drying the dishes. While these chores must be done and are good responsibilities for children to have, a great deal of enjoyment and learning are related to the food preparation in the kitchen. Hook your child on cooking—he'll use his skills all his life. And what a palatable way to practice reading, math, and science. Have him read the recipe to you so that you can make sure that it is being correctly interpreted. He can learn the measurements of ounces and pounds as well as the differences between beating and whipping, blending and stirring. He will learn about the various states of matter—solid, liquid, and gas from ice cubes. He will learn about mixing colors from working with food colorings. Spices can teach him different tastes. Boiling eggs and spaghetti and freezing desserts and stored foods can teach your child something of the Farenheit and Celsius scales. Changing substances such as flour into dough and dough into bread will show your child how outside forces (heat and water) will cause a chemical change to occur in certain substances.

Some helpful guidelines parents can use with their children in cooking experiences are

> At first, cooking should entail the elementary aspects such as washing of fruits and vegetables, cleaning corn on the cob, and mixing.
>
> Gradually allow your child to take on more and more responsibility in the kitchen as his skills improve.
>
> By the time children are in the sixth grade, they should be able to plan, prepare, serve, and clean up for the entire meal.
>
> Let them be creative after they have successfully mastered the skills of cooking by organizing their own menus and serving meals from foreign countries. (See pages 130-131 for other cooking activities.)

Some recommended cookbooks for children follow:

The Seabury Cook Book for Boys and Girls, by Eva Moore (Seabury, 1969), is for children in the second and third grades and contains easy-to-make recipes, from cinnamon toast to a full-course meal.

The Little Witch's Black Magic Cookbook, by Linda Glovach (Prentice-Hall, 1972), is also for second- and third-graders and contains many recipes for delectable snacks and brews.

Kids Are Natural Cooks, prepared by Parent's Nursery School (Houghton Mifflin, 1974), for children in the fourth, fifth, and sixth grades, is a children's guide to natural cooking, with suggestions for foods and drinks appropriate to each of the four seasons.

Betty Crocker's New Boys and Girls Cookbook, by Betty Crocker (Golden Press, 1965), illustrates safe cooking techniques and equipment and includes recipes for beverages, bread, sandwiches, salads, main dishes, and desserts.

Look Who's Cooking, by Marcie and John Carafoli (Follett, 1974), for children in the second, third, and fourth grades, encourages the young cook to experiment in the kitchen with creative recipes.

The Kid's Fifty-State Cookbook, by Aileen Paul (Doubleday, 1976), contains recipes and anecdotes concerning the enormous variety of cooking customs and eating habits in the United States.

Weather

Your child can become an amateur weather forecaster through a combination of his understanding of radio and television weather reports; his own, unaided observations, and observations derived from homemade weather instruments.

Every weather forecaster needs to know from what direction the wind is blowing. Your child can construct his weather vane by taking an eight- or ten-inch cardboard cylinder from a role of paper towels. Then have him cut a pointer and tail from other cardboard into the shape of an arrow head and tail. Place the pointer and tail at the ends of the cylinder by fitting them into slits made with a razor blade and then stapling them to the cylinder. Push a nail into the middle of the cylinder and then hammer the nail into a wooden shaft. A washer placed between the cylinder and the shaft will enable the arrow to turn more easily. Mount the vane in a place where the wind can hit it from any direction, and your child will have an instrument for measuring wind direction.

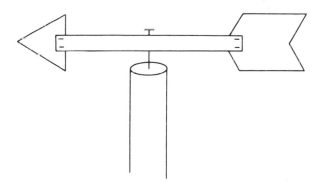

Wind is moving air. Sir Francis Beaufort, an early pioneer in weather reporting, established a scale for rating winds from calm to hurricane. Although it is not an exact scientific measurement, the Beaufort Scale will give your child a rough estimate of wind speed. Have him observe the wind conditions, describe them according to the scale, then check his estimate against what is said on the television weather report.

Scale Number	Wind Description	Wind Speed (mph)	Wind Effect
0	calm	under 1	smoke rises vertically, flags are limp
1	light air	1–3	drifting smoke shows wind direction
2	light breeze	4–7	leaves rustle, wind vanes turn
3	gentle breeze	8–12	flags blow straight out
4	moderate breeze	13–18	dust starts blowing
5	fresh wind	19–24	small trees sway
6	strong wind	25–31	large branches move, outdoor telephone wires whistle
7	high wind	32–38	it is hard to walk against the wind, whole trees sway
8	gale	39–46	it is extremely hard to walk against the wind, twigs break from trees
9	strong gale	47–54	branches break from trees, there is some slight damage to buildings
10	whole gale	55–63	trees are uprooted
11	violent storm	64–75	damage is widespread
12	hurricane	over 75	destruction is widespread

A rain gauge consisting of a soda bottle with a funnel placed in the mouth of the bottle and kept in the backyard or on a terrace will enable your child to keep records concerning the amount of rainfall (An easy way for your child to gauge his water collected with the actual rainfall is to compare the actual rainfall as reported on the weather report with the measured depth of the rainwater collected in his container. After three or four such comparisons he should be able to figure out the correct ratio quite accurately.)

the wettest day of the month

the wettest month of the year

Here are some good books for the amateur weather forecaster:

Let's Find Out About Weather by David Knight (Watts, 1967), *I Want to Be a Weatherman* by Eugene Baker (Children's Press, 1972), and *Wind Is to Feel* by Shirley Hatch (Coward, McCann and Geoghegan, 1973) are good books for second- and third-graders. Fourth-, fifth-, and sixth-graders might like *Projects With Air* by Seymour Simon (Watts, 1975), *Questions and Answers About Weather* by Jean Craig (Four Winds, 1969), and *What Will the Weather Be* by Julian May (Creative Educational, 1972).

Science—is everywhere, and parents can use it (as well as every other subject covered by the elementary school curriculum) to reinforce, through everyday living experiences, what their children learn in school. Making the world their classroom, parents can use their imagination to expand upon the activities in this book in order to help children learn through living and acting upon the things of their daily experiences.

Besides their school experiences, most children are involved in another experience that has virtually catapulted them into different dimensions, cultures, life-styles, values, and awarenesses. That experience is television, and parents can use this medium, too, as a means of reinforcing what children learn in school.

8

Television

Some Words About the Tube

Let's face it, television is a "turn-on" for children. All the arguments in the world are not going to convince most ten-year-olds that reading and studying are more important than "The Six Million Dollar Man" or "Charlie's Angels." Who doesn't like television? From beauty pageants to a close look at the wild, from sports to Shakespeare, from cartoons to soap operas, television has something for everyone, of every age, belief, nationality, income, wish, whim, and taste. It's Howard Johnson's twenty-eight flavors in a tube, and it sells like the Hula Hoop, the Frisbee, and the skateboard, except for one difference — television is here to stay. Its attraction and appeal is not going to decrease; it's going to increase.

Instead of throwing up their hands in despair, parents can use this medium to further their children's learning. By setting limits for its use, by understanding its inherent potential as a learning experience as well as its possible negative effects, parents can use TV as an activity for reinforcing school learning.

Among the positive aspects of television for children are these:

TV can present to the child all aspects of social interaction — love, hate, competition, friendship, death, sickness, work, and play.

TV can introduce the child to different cultures, nationalities, and environments that will help him learn about the world in which we live.

174

TV can stimulate conversation and enrich the speaking vocabulary of children.

TV can inform the child of local, national, and international news events.

TV programs can stimulate the child to learn more about the subject that was viewed.

TV can introduce the child to the various careers, sports, actors, political leaders, and historical figures.

TV can provide entertainment for your child.

Among the negative aspects of television for children are these:

TV can make passive listeners out of children, hypnotically tuning them in to images that require zero exercise of their thinking ability.

TV can minimize important physical activity for children by keeping them indoors instead of playing outside.

TV can divert children from their schoolwork and from reading in general.

TV can negatively influence children concerning worldwide events and living situations through the presentation of half facts and false realities.

It is important that parents establish certain limits on television viewing by children. Some guidelines for establishing these limits might be

Set a time limit for the number of hours TV viewing is allowed per day.

Make sure that all homework and household chores are completed *before* the child turns on the television.

Select good television programs for your children to watch. Children's shows, travelogs, nature shows, documentaries, the news, historical and artistic presentations can be enjoyable learning activities for children. Consult the *TV Guide* or your local newspaper for worthwhile programs *before* the set is turned on.

Don't use the television as a baby-sitter for your child. Instead, let him participate in whatever you are doing or give him a book, a game, or pen and paper to work with.

Try to watch programs with your child so that you can discuss them together.

Ask yourself and have your child ask himself, "Is there a valid reason for watching this show?" If an honest answer cannot be found, then have your child do something else.

Almost every television viewer, at one time or another, has caught himself being slowly drawn into a semitrance while watching TV. This powerful hypnotic effect is especially forceful on children. It can be seen in the child's eyes taking on a glassy film, the lower jaw hanging listlessly, and a total inattention to any outside stimuli. During this time your child is literally "out-of-it." He is not acting, he is passive, he is not aware of what he is doing, and is very often not even aware of what is happening on the screen. Most of all, when he is in this state, he is not learning.

Children learn best by doing, by taking part in experience in some way. The child must act or interrelate in some way with the subject matter. Such interaction is always evident in learning experiences. When your child is reading, he is using his mind and his eyes; when he is writing, he is using his mind, his eyes, and his hands; and when he is conversing, he is using his mind, his eyes, and his mouth. In short, he is personally involved with the subject matter.

The hypnotic state that television can induce can be circumvented by having your child focus on certain learning objectives as he watches. You can make the basically passive television experience into an active one of conscious interaction by stimulating your child with questions and problems for him to solve as he is watching, as well as activities for him to do before or after the program is viewed. Give him a *paper and pencil* to write down answers to questions such as names of characters, plot, factual information stated, type of sales pitch seen on commercials, as well as questions related to specific programs such as: "In this program that takes place on the prairie almost one hundred years ago list how the people traveled, methods of communication, and modes of dress." *Converse with him* about the program during the commercials as well as after the show, making him aware that he can view programs, actors, direction, setting, dialogue, and presentation of facts with a good critical eye. *Verbalize your thoughts*, that is, talk back to the tube whenever a character or announcer makes a ridiculous or meaningless statement. Although this may sound funny, the value of this verbalization will teach your child many things:

> that everything that is said on TV is not real, honest, or truthful
>
> that you do not agree with many things that are said on television
>
> that you are thinking critically as you watch the program, and your response is the verbalization of your thoughts
>
> that television does not have to be a totally passive experience for the viewer, that any intelligent viewer will react to television in a critical fashion, and that television can be an avenue of dialogue between the viewer and the announcer or the viewer and other viewers.

Learning Activities from Television

Television Related Activities For Younger Children

1. Shows such as "Sesame Street" can be a part of the daily routine of the child during which time parent and child view the program together and then talk about the different subjects in the show.

2. Have your child repeat a story in the show, naming the characters. This provides practice in concentration and retention.

3. If you have a color television set, you can teach the names of the colors while you and your child watch a show.

4. Have your child imitate the actions of the main characters in the show.

5. Make puppets and act out the story with your child.

6. During commercials help your child expand his imagination by asking him leading questions, such as "What would you do to capture the criminal?" or "How do you think the story will end?"

7. Watch for specials concerning geographical regions and different cultures throughout the world that will be shown on TV and borrow books from the library on these topics so that you can read them with your child before and after the show.

8. Watch for entertainment specials such as Walt Disney programs, Charlie Brown specials, National Geographic specials, and holiday presentations that have special appeal to children.

9. There is no better way to teach your child how to tell time than by using the time of his favorite television programs as a base. Make sure he looks at the clock at the beginning and end of each show and states the time. He can draw a "Time Book" that includes the name of the show, day, and a picture of a clock to indicate what time the show was aired.

10. Select books from the library on topics that the child especially enjoyed on television.

Television-Related Activities For Older Children

1. Have your child write summaries of any shows he watches in his own "Television Book," in which he also records the name of the show, the time and date of the show, and his criticism of it.

2. Teach your child to be a good critical viewer of dramatic programs by telling him to write a report that includes statements concerning the following information: Who were the main characters in the show? Were they good actors and actresses? Was it an adventure show, a mystery, a comedy, a tragedy, and what elements made it so? If you were the director how would you have improved the show?

3. The child can write a news report concerning one of the adventure or mystery movies he has viewed. Have him borrow the script of the fictional record broadcast by Orson Welles called *The War of the Worlds* from the library as a sample of a fictional radio broadcast.

4. Have your child analyze the news broadcasts of two different stations, looking for examples of bias or misleading use of facts. Make your child aware that out of an entire speech only a few short minutes may be shown, and the broadcast may present not what is most important but rather what is most exciting. It is important to see through opinions and to get at the truth.

5. After watching a TV drama involving social conflict, discuss with your child how the behavior of the characters in the show was affected by social or group pressure.

6. Have the child write his own *TV Guide*, based on the programs he regularly watches indicating the nature of each show (drama, situation-comedy, travelog, exposé, documentary), the time it is presented, the audience for whom it is intended, and a critique of the program.

7. While watching news programs and documentaries, ask your child to differentiate between statements of fact, fiction, and opinion. Are the facts clear? Are definite conclusions stated or implied? Remember, a fact isn't true just because it was stated on television.

8. While listening to talk shows, ask your child to list the points that should be questioned for further evidence.

9. After listening to a political or editorial talk, have your child summarize it, giving the main idea and two or three ways the orator substantiated his argument.

10. Listen for bias in newscasts concerning "loaded" words, exaggeration, statements of opinion or statements of prediction that are presented as fact and discuss these with the child.

11. Get your child to write a TV script that includes characters, setting of each scene, and dialogue.

12. Ask your child to analyze television programs using the following criteria:

Is there violence in the program?

Is there a social message in the program? What is it?

Is there a message of personal value?

Does the program contribute to intellectual growth?

Is the program beneficial as a means of relaxation?

13. Discuss violence on TV together as seen in movies, series, news, Westerns, horror movies, science fiction, comedies, war pictures. Was the violence used to make a point or was it merely sensationalism?

14. Have your child watch an exposé and list five statements of fact and five statements of opinion.

15. Have your child view commercials critically, asking such questions as

What have they really said about the product?

Have they given any proof about what they said?

Does the famous person who is selling the product in the commercial really know about it?

Even if something is a leading seller, does that mean that it is good for you?

What other sources can you go to in order to learn about a product?

16. Situation-comedies can be viewed critically, too. Ask your child to think about the following questions:

Are the characters real?

Do you learn more about the characters each week?

Does the action reflect life?

Why is this funny? Are the jokes original or have I heard them before?

17. Do the same thing with historical dramas. These shows that are based on history should not be accepted as absolute truth. What seems real and what doesn't? Where can one go to check on the facts?

Besides these general TV activities, the television experience can be used for specific learning reinforcement in the areas of language arts, math, social studies, and science. The remainder of this section deals with specific activities for each learning area.

Language Arts

Language Arts is about one thing—communication. Whenever you want your child to talk with you but you are stuck for an idea or topic, ask him "What is your favorite program?" and 99 percent of the time you will receive an excited reply.

Get to know your child's favorite programs by watching them with him, and you will have more than enough sources of information to lead him into discussions on other topics as well as using those programs as examples to answer the many questions posed by your child.

Most children can sing the theme songs of at least one or two of their favorite shows. Have your child sing them for the entire family, encouraging him to sing with expression, gestures, and a dash of humor.

For vocabulary development have your child keep a pad and pencil with him as he views the program to write down any words that he hears during the show that he does not understand. During the commercials he can look them up in the dictionary.

If your child doesn't like to read, buy some books in paperback or comic strip form that relate to his favorite programs. *The Waltons*, *Six Million Dollar Man*, and *Nancy Drew Mysteries* can turn many lethargic learners into voracious readers.

Have your child write letters to his favorite performers asking them questions about acting, singing, television careers, and other areas of entertainment.

"THE CRITIC'S REVIEW"   Have your child keep a critical review of each show he watches. It need not be long—a half page to a page— giving the following information:

Name of show

Time and day of presentation

Type of show (drama, situation-comedy, news, adventure, documentary)

Main characters, plot, and theme

New vocabulary words

Sponsors of show

Why the show was good or bad

(By having him keep such a log for each show, you will force your child to take an active part in the television viewing experience. He can write up the required information during the commercials and keep them together in a notebook or folder; they can then be read to the entire family.)

STORY WRITING   Have your child draw a scene from his favorite TV program and write a story about what is happening. A short script including dialogue, setting, and plot can be included by older children. Younger children can draw the picture, color it, and then dictate the story to the parent, who writes it down.

TALK SHOWS   As you view a talk show with your child, have him list additional questions that he would ask the individual if he was giving the interview.

Math

KEEPING SCORE   Whenever your child is viewing a sports program, have him be the official scorekeeper. This does not mean simply adding up the runs or points but including the players, number of fouls, errors, ball changeovers, sets won, and any other additional information relative to the sport being viewed. Have him borrow library books or write to the specific sports associations to find out how scoring sheets are kept for each particular game.

MOTIVATION   When you help your child with his math schoolwork, use the characters of his favorite television shows in the math problems.

> EXAMPLE: "The Six Million Dollar Man had only five minutes to save the hostages. He was ten miles away from them. How fast did he have to run in order to get to them on time?"

Social Studies

Television shows are full of social studies learning experiences. Family shows, movies, sports, news broadcasts, and panel discussions can provide a wealth of interesting information for a child.

MOVIES AND SHOWS ABOUT THE PAST   Have your child, when viewing shows about the past, compare the past to the present in terms of the following:

> methods of communication
>
> ways of travel
>
> types of entertainment
>
> modes of dress
>
> types of government
>
> food and housing
>
> jobs and careers
>
> values and life-styles
>
> religious and political beliefs

SPORTS   Discuss with your child the value of sports as entertainment, competitive achievement, and big-business money-making propositions for the competitors, owners, sponsors, and television stations.

Compare in terms of their dispositions players who win with players who lose. Some lose gracefully and with pride, whereas others lose dishonorably. Who are the great sports figures in the history of the different sports? What characteristics make up champions? Who are your child's favorite male and female sports figures? Use the newspaper to read about different sports events taking place on television. Have the child borrow library books about his favorite sports figures and read them before or after viewing these people on television.

One famous sportsman said, "Winning is the only thing." Discuss with your child the philosophy behind this statement. What is winning? Does one always have to win to be happy?

CAREERS   Television programs abound in information concerning the various careers in our society — a policeman, doctor, journalist, lawyer, teacher, detective, undercover agent, politician, mechanic, psychologist, psychiatrist, secretary, housewife, waiter, and movie star, to name just a few. You might also point out that there are important careers in life that receive little attention on TV.

Have your child write down as much information as possible concerning the career that the show concerns. Then have him borrow library books on the various careers to find out the requirements of each career, monetary considerations, as well as potential disadvantages involved in each career.

Science

Watch for specials concerning energy, health, space exploration, the oceans and other types of environments, life in the wild, as well as science fiction and adventure shows.

Watch the news, especially the weather. Have your child write to the weather broadcaster asking him questions about the weather report.

Before viewing a show on animal life or some other science subject, have your child look up the subject in the encyclopedia and compare this knowledge with that presented in the show. Have him list the facts he learned from the television show.

Epilogue

When our children become sick, we take them to the doctor; when they get cavities, we take them to the dentist. These professionals treat them and cause them to return to proper health. But proper health is actually a daily activity, and it is the job of parents, by providing the right food, clothing, and shelter on a daily basis, to see to it that their children remain healthy physically. By caring for their emotional needs of love and affection on a daily basis, parents also see to it that their children are happy individuals. Parents must do the same for their children's mental growth. Although the school is there to provide an educational foundation for children and to serve as the formal educator, parents must assume the role of informal educator in order to assure that their children fulfill their potential mentally as well as physically and emotionally. And when this occurs, when parents become aware of the very important role they play in their children's educational development as well as their physical and emotional development, when parents help their children to love learning out of respect for and interest in all things, when parents work with educators in a spirit of sharing this great task of educating a human being to lead a happy and successful life, and when children accept the fact that they are responsible for their schoolwork and their learning also, then what other result could possibly come about than—Successful Children!

Bibliography

Language Arts

Prekindergarten/Kindergarten

Agatha's Alphabet, by Lucy Floyd and Kathryn Lasky (Rand McNally, 1975).
All Butterflies, by Marcia Brown (Scribner, 1974).
Anno's Alphabet: An Adventure in Imagination, by Anno Mitsumasa (Crowell, 1974).
Bruno Bear's Bedtime Book, by Kathleen Daly (Strawberry/Larousse, 1976).
The Busy Book, by Ali Mitgutsch (Golden Press, 1976).
The Charlie Brown Dictionary, by Charles Schultz (Scholastic, 1975).
Early Words, by Richard Scarry (Random, 1976).
The Gingerbread Boy, illustrated by Paul Galdone (Seabury, 1975).
Grosset Starter Picture Dictionary (Grosset & Dunlap, 1975).
Grover and the Everything in the Whole Wide World Museum, by Norman Stiles and Daniel Wilcox (Random, 1974).
Henny Penny, by William Stobbs (Follett, 1968)
High Diddle Diddle, by Robert Propper (Museum of Modern Art, 1975).
The Little Engine That Could, by Watty Piper (Platt and Munk, 1976).
The Look Book, by Nicholas Tucker (Penguin, 1975).
The Mother Goose Book, (Random, 1976).
My Pictionary, by W. Greet, M. Monroe, and A. Schiller (Lothrop, 1970).
The Night Before Christmas, by Clement C. Moore (Lippincott, 1954).
Over, Under and Through, and Other Spatial Concepts, by Tana Hoban (Macmillan, 1973).
The Parade, by Kjell Ringi (Watts, 1975).
The Sesame Street Book of Letters (Little, Brown, 1970).
The Sesame Street Book of Opposites with Zero Mostel, by George Mendoza (Platt and Munk, 1974).
The Three Bears and 15 Other Stories, selected by Anne Rockwell (Crowell, 1975).

Grades 1 and 2

The Alphabet Tree, by Leo Lionni (Pantheon, 1968).
Alphabet World, by Barry Miller (Macmillan, 1971).

The Charlie Brown Dictionary, by Charles Schultz (Scholastic, 1975).
Christmas in the Woods, by Frances Frost (Harper and Row, 1976).
Circus, by Dick Bruna (Two Continents, 1975).
City A B C's, by Michael Deasy (Walker, 1974).
Fooling Around With Words, by Ruthven Tremain (Greenwillow, 1976).
Funniest Storybook Ever, by Richard Scarry (Random, 1972).
Goggles!, by Ezra Jack Keats (Macmillan, 1969).
The Golden Picture Dictionary, by Lucille Ogle and Tina Thoburn (Golden
    Press, 1976).
Jack Kent's Fables of Aesop, by Jack Kent (Parents, 1972).
Mr. Tall and Mr. Small, by Barbara Brenner (Young Scott Books, 1966).
My First Picture Dictionary, by W. Greet (Lothrop, 1970).
Pooh's Alphabet Book, by A.A. Milne (Dutton, 1975).
Thorndike Barnhart Beginning Dictionary, by E.L. Thorndike and Clarence
    Barnhart (Doubleday, 1972).

Grades 3 and 4

Beauty and the Beast, retold by Philippa Pearce (Crowell, 1972).
Biggest Riddle Book in the World, by Joseph Rosenbloom (Sterling, 1976).
Cinderella or The Little Glass Slipper, by Charles Perrault (Walck, 1970).
Definitions, by Charles Keller (Prentice-Hall, 1976).
The Fairy Tale Treasury, by Virginia Haveland (Coward, 1972).
Fairy Tales from Many Lands, by Arthur Rackham (Viking, 1974).
Free to Be . . . You and Me, by Marlo Thomas, ed. by Carole Hart (McGraw-
    Hill, 1974).
Girls and Boys Write-A-Letter Book, by Stan Tuson (Grosset & Dunlap, 1971).
Grimm's Fairy Tales, by Jacob Grimm (Viking, 1973).
The Hare and the Tortoise, by Jean de La Fontaine (Watts, 1966).
Hoke's Jokes, Cartoons and Funny Things, by Helen Hoke (Watts, 1973).
The Improbable Book of Records, by Quentin Blake (Atheneum, 1976).
More Fables of Aesop, by Jack Kent (Parents, 1974).
My World of Fairy Tales, by Jane Carruth (Rand McNally, 1976).
The Ox of the Wonderful Horns, and Other African Folktales, by Ashley
    Bryan (Atheneum, 1971).
The Pooh Get-Well Book, by Virginia Ellison (Dutton, 1973).
Scott Foresman Beginning Dictionary, by E.L. Thorndike and Clarence Barn-
    hart (Scott, Foresman, 1976).
Sports and Games in Verse and Rhyme, by Allen and Leland Jacobs (Garrard,
    1975).
The Story of Snow White and the Seven Dwarfs, by Jacob Grimm (Walck,
    1973).
Witch Poems, Daisy Wallace, ed. (Holiday House, 1976).

Grades 5 and 6

Aesop's Fables, trans. by Vernon Jones (Watts, 1969).
American Indian Fairy Tales, by Margaret Compton (Dodd, Mead, 1971).

The Big Book of Stories from Many Lands, by Rhoda Power (Watts, 1969).
The Christopher Robin Story Book, by A.A. Milne (Dutton, 1966).
Creative Plays and Programs for Holidays, by Rowena Bennett (Plays, 1966)
A Father Reads to His Children, An Anthology of Prose and Poetry, Orville
    Prescott, ed. (Dutton, 1965).
Favorite Fairy Tales in Czechoslovakia, . . . Denmark, by Ethna Sheehan
    (Dodd, Mead).
Folk and Fairy Tales from Around the World, by Ethna Sheehan (Dodd,
    Mead, 1970).
Haiku: The Mood of Earth, by Ann Atwood (Scribner, 1971).
The Home Book of Quotations: Classical and Modern, Burton Stevenson, ed.
    (Dodd, Mead, 1967).
How to Write a Story, by Bentz Plagemann (Lothrop, 1971).
In Other Words; A Beginning Thesaurus, by Cabell Greet (Lothrop, 1968).
Italy, by Virginia Haveland (Little, Brown).
Japan, by Virginia Haveland (Little, Brown).
Jokes, Puns and Riddles, by David Clark (Doubleday, 1968).
Macmillan Dictionary for Children, W. Halsey and C. Morris, eds. (Macmil-
    lan, 1975).
Medallion World Atlas (Hammond, 1975).
Poems of Lewis Carroll, selected by Myra Livingston (Crowell, 1973).
The Rime of the Ancient Mariner, by Samuel Coleridge, illustrated by Walter
    Hodges (Coward, 1971).
Science Fiction Tales, Roger Elwood, ed. (Rand McNally, 1973).
The Story of the Dictionary, by Robert Kraske (Harcourt, 1975).
Sweden, by Virginia Haveland (Little, Brown).
Webster's New World Dictionary for Young Readers, David Guralnik, ed.
    (World, 1971).
You Come Too, by Robert Frost (Holt, 1967).

Mathematics

Pre-Kindergarten/Kindergarten

The Berenstain Bears Counting Book, by Stanley and Janice Berenstain
    (Random, 1976).
Count on Calico Cat, by Donald Charles (Childrens Press, 1974).
Count the Cats, by Erika Weihs (Doubleday, 1976).
Let's Count, by Adelaide Holl (Addison-Wesley, 1976).
My Measure It Book, by Vivian Bennett (Grosset & Dunlap, 1975).
Numbers, by Jan Pienkowski (Harvey, 1974).
Odd One Out, by Rodney Peppe (Viking, 1974).
One is For the Sun, by Lenore and Erik Blegvad (Harcourt, 1968).
One More and One Less, by Giulio Maestro (Crown, 1974).
One, Two, Three, by Marc Brown (Little, Brown, 1976).
The Sesame Street Book of Puzzles (Little, Brown, 1970).
The Sesame Street Book of Shapes (Little, Brown, 1970).

Shapes, by Jan Pienkowski (Harvey, 1974).
Sizes, by Jan Pienkowski (Harvey, 1974).
Teddy Bears 1 to 10, by Susanna Gretz (Follett, 1969).
Ten Bears in My Bed, by Stanley Mack (Pantheon, 1974).
Ten Little Elephants, by Robert Leydenfrost (Doubleday, 1975).

Grades 1 and 2

Brian Wildsmith's 1, 2, 3's, by Brian Wildsmith (Watts, 1965).
Circles, by Mindel Sitomer (Crowell, 1971).
Estimation, by Charles Linn (Crowell, 1970).
Let's Find Out About Addition, by David Whitney (Watts, 1966).
Long, Short, High, Low, Thin, Wide, by James Fey (Crowell, 1971).
Many is How Many, by Illa Podendorf (Childrens Press, 1970).
Mathematical Games for One or Two, by Mannis Charosh (Crowell, 1972).
Numbers: A First Counting Book, by Robert Allen (Platt and Munk, 1968).
One, Two, Three, by Ulf Lofgren (Addison-Wesley, 1973).
One, Two, Three For the Library, by Mary Little (Atheneum, 1974).
The Parade of Shapes, by Sylvia Tester (Child's World, 1976).
Right Angles, by Jo Phillips (Crowell, 1972).
Square is a Shape, by Sharon Lerner (Lerner, 1970).
Strait is a Line, by Sharon Lerner (Lerner, 1970).
Three Sides and The Round One, by Margaret Friskey (Children's Press, 1973).
Weighting and Balancing, by Jane Srivastava (Crowell, 1970).

Grades 3 and 4

Arithmetic in Verse and Rhyme, by Allen Jacobs (Garrard, 1971).
Bigger and Smaller, by Robert Froman (Crowell, 1971).
The Easy Book of Division, . . . of Fractions, . . . of Numbers and Numerals, by David C. Whitney (Watts).
Fractions are Parts of Things, by Richard Dennis (Crowell, 1971).
I've Got Your Number, by John and Olive Berg (Holt, 1965).
The Life of Numbers, by Fernando Krahn (Simon & Schuster, 1970).
Measurements and How We Use Them, by Tillie Pine (McGraw-Hill, 1974).
The Metric System, by William Shimek (Lerner, 1965).
Name, Sets and Numbers, by Jeanne Bendick (Watts, 1971).
Odds and Evens, by Thomas O'Brien (Crowell, 1971).
Sets and Numbers for the Very Young, by Irving Adler (Day, 1969).
Shapes, by Jeanne Bendick (Watts, 1968).
Shapes, Sides, Curves and Corners, by Illa Podendorf (Children's Press, 1970).
Straight Lines, Parallel Lines, Perpendicular Lines, by Mannis Charosh (Crowell, 1970).
Venn Diagrams, by Robert Froman (Crowell, 1972).

Grades 5 and 6

The Calendar, by Irving Adler (John Day, 1967).
Circles and Curves, by Arthur Razzell (Doubleday, 1968).
Computers, Tools for Today, by Claude De Rossi (Children's Press, 1972).
Directions and Angles, by Irving Adler (John Day, 1969).
Integers: Positive and Negative, by Irving Adler (John Day, 1972).
Lines and Shapes, by Solveig Russell (Walck, 1965).
Measuring, by Jeanne Bendick (Watts, 1971).
Meet the Meters!, by Glenn Leslie (Ballantine, 1976).
Metric, by Miriam Schlein (Harcourt, 1975).
Think Metric, by Franklyn Branley (Crowell, 1972).
What is Symmetry?, by Mindel Sitomer (Crowell, 1970).

Social Studies

Pre-Kindergarten/Kindergarten

Bear By Himself, by Geoffrey Hayes (Harper and Row, 1976).
The Chicken Child, by Margaret Hartelius (Doubleday, 1975).
Country Noisy Book, by Margaret Brown (Harper and Row, 1976).
Dick Bruna's Animal Book, by Dick Bruna (Two Continents, 1976).
Fish for Supper, by M.B. Goffstein (Dial, 1976).
Grandma is Somebody Special, by Susan Goldman (Whitman, 1976).
I Have Four Names for My Grandfather, by Kathryn Lasky (Little, Brown, 1976)
I Love My Mother, by Paul Zindel (Harper and Row, 1975).
Let's Take a Walk, by Stu Graves (Grosset & Dunlap, 1975).
Nicky Goes to the Doctor, by Richard Scarry (Golden Press, 1972).
The Sesame Street Book of People and Things (Little, Brown, 1970).
Tunafish Sandwiches, by Patty Wolcott (Addison-Wesley, 1975).

Grades 1 and 2

Behind the Wheel, by Ed Koren (Holt, 1972).
City in the Winter, by Eleanor Schick (Macmillan, 1970).
The Creation, illustrated by Jo Spier (Doubleday, 1970).
Hanukkah, by Norma Simon (Crowell, 1966).
Have You Seen Houses, by Joanne Oppenheim (Young Scott Books, 1972).
Hop Aboard! Here We Go, by Richard Scarry (Golden Press, 1972).
I Know a Postman, by Lorraine Henriod (Putnam, 1967).
I Know a Telephone Operator, by J. Evans (Putnam, 1971).
Let's Find Out About the City, by Valerie Pitt (Watts, 1968).
Let's Find Out About Halloween, by Paulette Cooper (Watts, 1972).
Miguel's Mountain, by Bill Binzen (Coward, 1968).

On and Off the Street, by Bob Adelman and Susan Hall (Viking, 1970).
On the Beat; Policeman at Work, by Barry Robinson (Harcourt, 1968).
Rosie's Walk, by Pat Hutchins (Macmillan, 1968).
The Three Little Pigs, by Paul Galdone, (Seabury, 1970).
The Town Mouse and the Country Mouse, by Paul Galdone (McGraw-Hill, 1971).

Grades 3 and 4

About Doctors of Long Ago, by Naida Dickson (Melmont, 1972).
Airports, U.S.A., by Lou Jacobs (Elk Grove, 1967).
Careers in a Bank, by Mary Davis (Lerner, 1973).
Careers in a Medical Center, by Mary Davis (Lerner, 1973).
Chicanos: Mexicans in the United States, by Patricia Martin (Parents, 1971).
Cities Old and New, by William Wise (Parents, 1973).
Computers, by Melvin Berger (Coward, 1972).
The Farm, by Solveig Russell (Parents, 1970).
Finding Out About the Past, by Mae Freeman (Random, 1967).
The Food You Eat, by John Mair (Evans, 1973).
How People Earn and Use Money, by Muriel Stanek (Benefic, 1968).
I Know a Newspaper Reporter, by Lorraine Henriod (Putnam, 1971).
The Jewish New Year, by Molly Cone (Crowell, 1966).
Let's Find Out About Communications; . . . the Community, by Valerie Pitt (Watts, 1973).
Let's Go to a Jetport, by Barbara Rich (Putnam, 1973).
The Pirate Book, by Mickie Davidson (Random, 1965).
The Story of Things, by Frank Jupo (Prentice-Hall, 1972).
What Happens at a Newspaper, by Arthur Shay (Reilly and Lee, 1972).

Grades 5 and 6

An Album of Women in American History, by Claire and Leonard Ingraham (Watts, 1972).
The American Heritage Book of Natural Wonders (Am. Heritage, 1972).
Around the World in 80 Dishes, by Polly Van der Linde (Scroll, 1971).
Art and Archeology, by Shirley Glubok (Harper and Row, 1966).
The Art of Africa, by Shirley Glubok (Harper and Row, 1965).
Bible for Children, by J. Klink (Westminster, 1967).
Electing Our Presidents, by Helen Stone (Garrard, 1970).
Facts About the 50 States, by Sue Brandt (Watts, 1970).
Feeding the City, by Beulah Tannenbaum and Myra Stillman (McGraw-Hill, 1971).
The First Book of Facts and How to Find Them, by David C. Whitney (Watts, 1966).
The Grosset World Atlas, by (Grossett & Dunlap, 1973).
Growing a Garden Indoors and Out, by Catherine Cutler (Lothrop, Lee & Shepard, 1973).

Historical American Landmarks, by C. B. Colby (Coward, 1968).
How the World's First Cities Began, by Arthur Gregor (Dutton, 1967).
Illustrated Atlas For Young America (Hammond, 1967).
Milk, Butter and Cheese, the Story of Dairy Products, by Carolyn Meyer (Morrow, 1974).
Save the Earth! An Ecology Handbook for Kids, by Betty Miles (Knopf, 1974).
Skyscraper Goes Up, by Carter Harman (Random, 1973).
The United Nations, by Edna Epstein (Watts, 1971).
What A State Governor Does, by Roy Hoopes (John Day, 1973).
What Happens When You Spend Money, by Arthur Shay (Reilly and Lee, 1970).

Science

Pre-Kindergarten/Kindergarten

Air is All Around You, by F. Branley (Crowell, 1962).
Crash! Bang! Boom, by Peter Spier (Doubleday, 1972).
Dick Bruna's Animal Book, by Dick Bruna (Two Continents, 1976).
Earth and Sky, by Mona Dayton (Harper and Row, 1969).
Floating and Sinking, by F. Branley (Crowell, 1967).
Hi, New Baby, by Andrew Andry (Simon and Schuster, 1970).
Hot As an Ice Cube, by P. Balestrino (Crowell, 1971).
How Puppies Grow, by Millicent Selsam (Four Winds, 1971).
The Life Picture Book of Animals, by Robert Mason (Time-Life, 1969).
The Little Man in Winter, by Walburga Attenberger (Random, 1972)
Machines, by Anne Rockwell (Macmillan, 1972).
One Day in the Garden, by M. Vasiliu (John Day, 1969).
One Wide River to Cross, by Barbara Emberley (Prentice-Hall, 1966).
A Rainbow of My Own, by Don Freeman (Viking, 1966).
Seasons, by John Burningham (Bobbs-Merrill, 1969).
See My Garden Grow, by Jane Moncure (Child's World, 1976).
The Snowy Day, by Ezra Jack Keats (Scholastic, 1972).
Some of Us Walk, Some Fly, Some Swim, by Michael Frith (Beginner Books, 1971).
Tiny Seed, by E. Carle (Crowell, 1970).
Water is Wet, by Sally Cartwright (Coward, 1973).
What Floats, by Mary Brewer (Child's World, 1976).
Wheels, by Ellie Simmons (McKay, 1969).
Wind is Air, by Mary Brewer (Child's World, 1975).
The Zoo in My Garden, by Chiyoko Nakatani (Crowell, 1973).

Grades 1 and 2

ABC Science Experiments, by Harry Milgrom (Crowell-Collier, 1970).
Adventures With A Party Plate, by Harry Milgrom (Dutton, 1968).

Animal Friends, by Phoebe Dunn (Creation Educational, 1971).
At Last to the Ocean, by Joel Rothman (Crowell-Collier, 1971).
The Brook, by Carol and Dick Carrick (Macmillan, 1967).
The Cave: What Lives There, by Andrew Bronin (Coward, 1972).
The Cloud Book, by Tomie De Paola (Holiday House, 1975).
Do You Know About Water?, by Mae Freeman (Random, 1970).
Eclipse: Darkness in Daytime, by Franklyn Branley (Crowell, 1973).
Exploring as You Walk in the Meadow, by Phyllis Busch (Lippincott, 1972).
Is This a Baby Dinosaur?, by Millicent Selsam (Harper and Row, 1971).
Lets Find Out About Weather, by David Knight (Watts, 1967).
Over in the Meadow, by Ezra Jack Keats (Four Winds, 1971).
Science Games, by Lawrence White (Addison-Wesley, 1975).
Small Worlds, A Field Trip Guide, by Helen Russell (Little, Brown, 1972).
Things Around Us, by Hubert Freestrom (Benefic, 1970).
Turtle Pond, by Bernice Freschet (Scribner, 1971).
What Floats?, by Mary Brewer (Children Press, 1976).
Who, What and When, by Illa Podendorf (Children Press, 1971).

Grades 3 and 4

The A-to-Z No-Cook Cookbook, by Felipe Rojas–Lombardi (Golden Press, 1974).
ABC's of the Ocean; . . . Ecology, by Isaac Asimov (Walker).
The Book of Magnets, by Mae Freeman (Four Winds, 1967).
The Book of the Milky Way Galaxy For You, by Franklyn Branley (Crowell, 1965).
By the Seashore, by Winifred Lubell (Parents, 1973).
Collecting Small Fossils, by Lois Hussey (Crowell, 1970).
Cup-and-Saucer Chemistry, by Nathan Shalit (Grosset & Dunlap, 1972).
Days in the Woods, by Harris Stone (Prentice-Hall, 1972).
Earth Through the Ages, by Philip Carona (Follet, 1968).
Everyday Wildflowers, by Gertrude Allen (Houghton Mifflin, 1965).
Exploring as You Walk in the City, by Phyllis Busch (Lippincott, 1972).
From Field to Forest, by Lawrence Ringle (World, 1970).
Hidden Animals, by Millicent Selsam (Harper and Row, 1969).
Let's Find Out About the Ocean, by David Knight (Watts, 1970).
Magnify and Find Out Why, by Julius Schwartz (McGraw-Hill, 1972).
Motion and Gravity, by Joanna Bendick (Watts, 1972).
The Seabury Cook Book for Boys and Girls, by Eva Moore (Seabury, 1969).
Table Top Science, by S. Fisher (National History, 1972).
A Walk in the Snow, by Phyllis Busch (Lippincott, 1971).
Weather All Around, by Tillie Pine (McGraw-Hill, 1966).
What is Science?, by John Scott (Parents, 1972).
A Zoo For You, by Winifred Lubell (Parents, 1970).

Grades 5 and 6

Atlas of Plant Life, by Herbert Edlin (John Day, 1973).
Birth, the Story of How You Came to Be, by Lionel Gendron (Dunlap, 1970).

City Rocks, City Blocks and the Moon, by Edward Gallob (Scribner, 1973).
Experiments, by Rocco Ferariola (Gerrard, 1965).
First Experiments With Gravity, by Harry Milgrom (Dutton, 1966).
A Guide to Nature Projects, by Ted Pettit (Norton, 1966).
How Did We Find Out About Electricity, by Isaac Asimov (Walker, 1973).
Into the Woods: Exploring the Forest Ecosystem, by Lawrence Pringle (Macmillan, 1973).
Man and Woman, by Julian May (Follett, 1969).
Projects With Plants, by Seymour Simon (Watts, 1973).
Science Experiments You Can Eat, by Vicki Cobb (Lippincott, 1972).
Science Projects in Ecology, by Seymour Simon (Holiday House, 1972).
Science Projects That Make Sense, by Harris Stone (McCall Pub., 1971).
Science in a Vacant Lot, by Seymour Simon (Viking, 1970).
Terrariums, by John Hoke (Watts, 1972).
This World of Wonder, by Hal Borland (Lippincott, 1973).
To the Ends of the Universe, by Isaac Asimov (Walker, 1967).
The Universe, by Herbert Zim (Morrow, 1973).
Windows on the World, by Anne White and Gerald Lietz (Garrard, 1965).

Crafts, Games, Recreation

Pre-Kindergarten/Kindergarten

Activities to Learn By, by Lilian and Godfrey Frankel (Sterling, 1974).
Art Activities for the Very Young, by F. Louis Hoover (Davis Pub., 1961).
The Big Book of Things to Do and Make, by Helen Fletcher (Random, 1961).
Child Learning Through Child Play, by I. Gordon (St. Martins, 1972).
Helping Young Children Learn, by E. Pitcher (Merrill, 1974).
I Saw a Purple Cow: and 100 Other Recipes for Learning, by Anne Cole (Little, Brown, 1972).
Making Easy Puppets, by Shari Lewis (Dutton, 1967).
A Pumpkin in a Pear Tree, by A. Cole, C. Haas, E. Heller and B. Weinberger (Little, Brown, 1976).

Grades 1 and 2

Clay-Dough, Play-Dough, by Goldie Chernoff (Walker, 1974).
Fantastic Toys, by Monika Beisner (Follett, 1973).
Kids Cooking With a Stove, by Aileen Paul (Doubleday, 1975).
Let's Make a Kite, by Jack Stokes (Walck, 1976).
The Little Witch's Black Magic Book of Games, by Linda Glovach (Prentice-Hall, 1974).
The Make-It, Play-It Game Book, by Roz Abisch and Boche Kaplan (Walker, 1975).
Mickey Mouse Make-It Book (Random, 1974).
Mobiles You Can Make, by Loretta Holz (Lothrop, 1975).
Pint-Size Fun, by Betsy Pflug (Lippincott, 1972).

Something to Make, Something to Talk About, by Martha Condit (Four
    Winds, 1976).
Start to Draw, by Ann Campbell (Watts, 1968).

Grades 3 and 4

Bag of Tricks, by James Razzi (Parents, 1971).
Charlie Brown's Super Book of Things to Do and Collect, by Charles Schultz
    (Random, 1975).
The Children's Book of Painting, by Lothar Kampmann (Van Nostrand,
    Reinhold, 1971).
The Complete Book of Baseball Cards, by Steve Clark (Grosset & Dunlap,
    1976).
Easy Does It, by James Razzi (Parents, 1969).
Easy to Make Puppets, by Freida Gates (Havery, 1976).
Everything Book, by Eleanor Vance (Golden Press, 1974).
Funny Magic, by Rose Wyler (Parents, 1972).
Games (and How to Play Them), by Anne Rockwell (Crowell, 1973).
Gargoyles, Monsters and Other Beasts, by Shay Rieger (Lothrop, 1972).
Hamsters, by Alvin and Virginia Silverstein (Lothrop, 1974).
Jewelry from Junk, by Helen Sattler (Lothrop, 1973).
The Kid's Kitchen Takeover, by Sara Stein (Workman, 1975).
The Little Kid's Craft Book, by Jackie Vermeer (Toplinger, 1973).
Make It with Felt, by Arden Newsome (Lothrop, 1972).
Paperfolding to Begin With, by Florence Temko (Bobbs-Merrill, 1968).
Simply Fun!, by James Razzi (Parents, 1968).
Steven Caney's Playbook, by Steven Caney (Workman, 1975).
*The You and Me Heritage Tree: Children's Craft from 21 American Tradi-
    tions,* by Phyllis and Noel Fiarotta (Workman, 1976).
You Can Make Seaside Treasures, by Louis Beetschen (Knopf, 1974).

Grades 5 and 6

Aquariums, by John Hoke (Watts, 1975).
Backpacking, by Tony Gibbs (Watts, 1975).
The Beachcomber's Book, by Bernice Kohn (Viking, 1970).
Beginning Stamp Collecting, by Bill Olcheski (Walck, 1975).
Bicycle Touring, by Irene Kleeberg (Watts, 1975).
Candles for Beginners to Make, by Alice Gilbreath (Morrow, 1975).
Card Games for Kids, by John Giannoni (Golden Press, 1973).
Carving: How to Carve Wood and Stone, by Harvey Weiss (Addison-Wesley,
    1975).
Cookie Art, by Sally Brewer (Schmitt, Hall and McCreary, 1972).
Costumes to Make, by Peggy Parish (Macmillan, 1970).
Do It Yourself Dinosaurs, by Brenda Morton (Taplinger, 1973).
Family Book of Crafts, by Louisa Hellegers (Sterling, 1973).
Fell's Guide to Hand Puppets, by Dorothy Richter (Fell, 1970).

Fifty Favorite Hobbies, by Arthur Liebers (Hawthorn, 1968).
Fun with Growing Things, by Joan Eckstein (Arion, 1975).
Kids Cooking Complete Meals, by Aileen Paul (Doubleday, 1975).
Lots of Fun to Cook, by Lise Marin (Collins-World, 1974).
Making and Using Finger Puppets, by Margaret-Hutchings (Toplinger, 1973).
Mobiles You Can Make, by Loretta Holy (Lothrop, 1975).
National Park Guide, by Michael Frome (Rand McNally, 1973).
Pack-O-Fun Craft Projects, by Edna Clapper (Hawthorn, 1972).
Paper Play, by Michael Grater (Taplinger, 1972).
Pets in a Jar, by Seymour Simon (Viking, 1975).
Photo Fun: An Idea Book for Shutterbugs, by David Webster (Webster, 1973).

Song, Rhyme and Poetry Books

Pre-Kindergarten/Kindergarten

Lavender's Blue, by Kathleen Lines and Harold Jones (Watts, 1966).
London Bridge is Falling Down, illustrated by Peter Spier (Doubleday, 1967).
Lullabies and Night Songs, by Alex Wilder (Harper and Row, 1965).
Mother Goose: A Treasury of Best-Loved Rhymes, Watty Piper, ed. (Platt and Munk, 1972).
The Night Before Christmas, by Clement C. Moore (Random, 1975).
Six Little Ducks, by Chris Conover (Crowell, 1976).
Songs the Sandman Sings, by Gwendolyn Reed (Atheneum, 1969).

Grades 1 and 2

The Baby's Song Book, by Elizabeth Poston (Crowell, 1971).
Cat and Mouse, a Book of Rhymes, by Rodney Peppe (Holt, 1973).
Every Child's Book of Nursery Songs, by Donald Mitchell (Crown, 1968).
Mother Goose, Eulalie Osgood Grover, ed. (Hubbard, 1915).
One Misty Moisty Morning: Rhymes from Mother Goose, pictures by Mitchell Miller (Farrar, Straus and Giroux, 1971).
The Sesame Street Song Book, by Joe Raposo and Jeffrey Moss (Simon and Schuster, 1971).
Sing Mother Goose, by Opal Wheeler (Dutton, 1945).

Grades 3 and 4

Chinese Mother Goose Rhymes, Robert Wyndham, ed. (World, 1968).
The Christopher Robin Book of Verse, by A.A. Milne (Dutton, 1967).
Favorite Poems for the Children's Hour, by Josephine Bouton (Platt and Munk, 1967).
The Fireside Book of Children's Songs, by Marie Winn (Simon and Schuster, 1966).

A Pocketful of Riddles, by William Wiesner (Dutton, 1966).
Riddle Me, Riddle Me, Ree, by Maria Leach (Viking, 1970).
The Wheels of the Bus Go Round and Round, by Nancy Larrick (Golden Gate
    Jr. Books, 1972).

Grades 5 and 6

The Gambit Book of Children's Songs, Donald Mitchell, comp. (Gambit,
    1970).
Glad Day, and Other Classical Poems for Children, by Ronald Himler (Put-
    nam, 1972).
The Laura Ingalls Wilder Songbook, Eugenia Garson, ed. (Harper and Row,
    1968).
Pick Me Up: A Book of Short Poems, William Cole, ed. (Macmillan, 1972).
Songs and Stories of the North American Indian, by Paul Glass (Grosset &
    Dunlap, 1968).
Songs of '76, by Oscar Brand (Evans, 1972).

Books for Parents Concerning Reading

The Development of Language and Reading in the Young Child, by Susanna
    Pflaum (Merrill, 1974).
How to Increase Reading Ability, by Albert Harris and Edward Sipay
    (McKay, 1975).
Reading Activities for Child Involvement, by Evelyn Spache (Allyn and Ba-
    con, 1976).
Reading Aids Through the Grades, by David Russell and Etta Karp (Teach-
    ers College Press, 1975).
The Teaching of Reading, by Martha Dallmann and others (Holt, 1974).

INDEX

198